Leading Economic Controversies of 1996

Leading Economic Controversies of 1996

EDWIN MANSFIELD
University of Pennsylvania

W. W. Norton & Company

NEW YORK   LONDON

To Beth and Ken

ALL RIGHTS RESERVED
PRINTED IN THE UNITED STATES OF AMERICA

This book is composed in ITC Baskerville
Composition by Com Com
Manufacturing by Haddon
Book design by Martin Lubin

Library of Congress Catalog in Publication Data
Leading economic controversies of 1996 / [edited by] Edwin Mansfield.
    p.   cm.
    1. United States—Economic policy—1993–   I. Mansfield, Edwin.
HC106.82.L4   1996
338.973'009'049—dc20   95-31638

ISBN 0-393-96955-X
W. W. Norton & Company, Inc.,
500 Fifth Avenue, New York, N.Y. 10110
W. W. Norton & Company Ltd.,
10 Coptic Street, London WC1A 1PU

1 2 3 4 5 6 7 8 9 0

Contents

PART NINE: **INTERNATIONAL TRADE POLICY**

PART TEN: **ECONOMIC REFORM IN EASTERN EUROPE**

Preface

Economics is an exciting subject—or it can be if it is taught properly. Obviously, one of the most important purposes of an elementary economics course is to get students interested in the subject, and this can best be done by showing them how the principles of economics can enable them to understand better the major economic issues of today. That in brief is the purpose of the second edition of this book, which focuses on ten central policy areas: (1) the distribution of income, (2) welfare reform, (3) competition on the information superhighway, (4) antitrust policy, (5) the environment, (6) promoting U.S. economic growth, (7) fiscal policy, (8) monetary policy, (9) international trade policy, and (10) economic reform in Eastern Europe. Over half of the articles included are new to this edition.

These policy areas play a major role in practically any elementary economics course. To arouse students' interest in each of these areas, this book presents contrasting (or in some cases, complementary) views by leading policy makers (like Al Gore, Alan Greenspan, Boris Yeltsin, and Alan Blinder), prominent scholars (like Gary Becker), and major business executives (like Robert Lutz), as well as government advisory groups like the President's Council of Economic Advisers. Each of the articles is at a level that is appropriate for the typical undergraduate. The articles, many of which are based on speeches, tend to be lighter in tone—and hence more palatable to students—than many other discussions of these issues. Also, it is worth noting that these articles are all very up-to-date, the publication dates being 1993, 1994, and 1995 (except in one case).

In each of the ten parts of this book, after the articles presenting different views of a particular issue, there are at least ten questions for analysis. These questions, which can form the basis for classroom discussion or homework exercises, are meant to provide an overview of the articles and to encourage the student to relate key points in the articles to the principles of economics.

This book was originally conceived as a supplement to *Economics U.S.A.,* Fourth Edition, but many instructors have used it to supplement other elementary economics textbooks; and some have used it alone.

E.M.

October 1995

PART ONE

THE

DISTRIBUTION

OF INCOME

Two of the big concerns of the mid-1990s have been the relatively slow rate of growth of real income in the United States and the growing inequality of incomes, but there has been considerable debate about what these trends mean and don't mean. The first article, by President Clinton's Council of Economic Advisers, attributes the slow growth of real income to a slowdown in productivity growth and the increase in inequality to increasing returns to education and experience. The second article, by the Republican members of the Joint Economic Committee of Congress, attacks some of the statistical evidence used to support the proposition that income inequality has increased. The third article contains the contrasting views of David Card and Alan Krueger, on the one hand, and Gary Becker, on the other, regarding the effects of increases in the minimum wage, a device sometimes advocated as a way to push up the wages of relatively unskilled workers.

Slowing Wage Growth and Widening Inequality

Laura D'Andrea Tyson

PRESIDENT CLINTON'S COUNCIL OF ECONOMIC ADVISERS*

In the last two decades, family income growth has stagnated and incomes have become more unequally distributed. In fact, the real incomes of the bottom 60 percent of American families were lower in the early 1990s than for the analogous families at the end of the 1970s. Underlying the rising disparity in the fortunes of American families has been a rise in labor market inequality that has shifted wage and employment opportunities in favor of the more educated and the more experienced. Less educated workers suffered substantial losses in real earnings during the 1980s. Here we consider the dimensions, and some likely causes, of slow income growth and widening inequality.

SLOW INCOME GROWTH

Income trends have been discouraging for about two decades—the median family today has virtually the same real income as the median family 20 years ago. This stagnation is a marked departure from the substantial income growth that occurred over previous generations.

From 1947 to 1973 the real income of the median American family in-

*This is an excerpt from the *Economic Report of the President* (Washington, DC: Government Printing Office, 1994).

CHART 1 Real Hourly Compensation and Wages

The growth of real compensation per hour and of real hourly wages has declined since 1973.

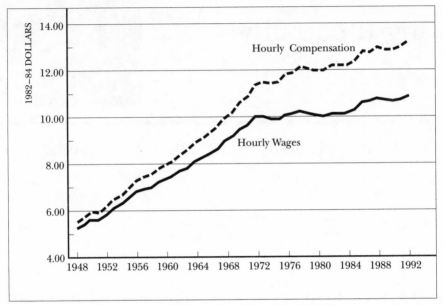

Note: Compensation and average hourly earnings deflated by CPI-U-X1.

Sources: Department of Commerce and Department of Labor.

creased by a robust 2.8 percent a year, more than doubling. In contrast, from 1973 to 1992 the income of the typical American family was essentially stagnant, rising by only 0.1 percent a year after adjusting for inflation. (The trend from 1979 to 1989—roughly equivalent years in the economic cycle—is similar.) At the pace of income growth from 1973 to 1992, it would take centuries for real median family income to double.

Although the labor force participation decisions of women and changes in the composition of families have affected family income, the major trends in family income are dominated by trends in real wages. Chart 1 shows the changes in wages and total hourly compensation, adjusted for inflation, since 1948. Both wages and compensation suffered abrupt slowdowns in growth rates around 1973.

BOX 1. **GROWING INEQUALITY OF EMPLOYMENT AND UNEMPLOYMENT**

The falling relative wages of those with less experience and schooling may explain, at least in part, some of the observed changes in employment-to-population ratios for certain demographic groups. The black and teenage populations tend to have less schooling than the average for all Americans. Consequently, the wages they command have fallen, making work less attractive. To the extent that the shift in demand away from less-educated workers is manifest in fewer available jobs instead of lower wages, these groups face higher unemployment rates as well.

GROWING INEQUALITY

Families have been affected unevenly by recent income trends. Real incomes at the top have increased smartly, real incomes at the middle have essentially stagnated, and real incomes at the bottom have fallen. Box 1 discusses the implications of these developments for employment and unemployment.

From 1973 to 1992, the average real income of the upper 20 percent of families rose 19 percent, or about 1 percent per year. This is well below the rate for the 1950s and 1960s, but far better than for the rest of the population. Between 1973 and 1992, the average income of the middle 20 percent of families rose a paltry 4 percent in real terms. Lower income families fared even worse. Among the bottom 20 percent of families, mean real income fell by 12 percent from 1973 to 1992. Chart 2 shows the growth of mean family incomes for different income groups over the periods before and after 1973. It makes clear just how abrupt the changes in the distribution of income growth have been. A trend toward greater equality in the 1960s and toward greater inequality in the 1970s and 1980s is apparent in both income and consumption measures of economic well-being. Rising inequality of family incomes during the 1980s is apparent in both pretax and posttax income measures.

EXPLAINING SLOW WAGE GROWTH

Stagnant wages and slow total compensation growth since the early 1970s largely reflect a substantial slowdown in productivity growth. [Productivity is defined as output per hour of labor.] From 1947 to 1973 productivity rose at a compound annual rate of 3.1 percent, and inflation-adjusted compensation per hour grew at a similar rate. From 1973 to 1979 the rate of productivity growth fell to an average of 0.8 percent a year, and compensation growth fell with it. Since 1979 the productivity growth rate has picked

CHART 2   Average Annual Growth of Mean Family Income by Income Quintile

Family incomes in all income groups grew more or less evenly, but slightly faster for lower income groups, before 1973.

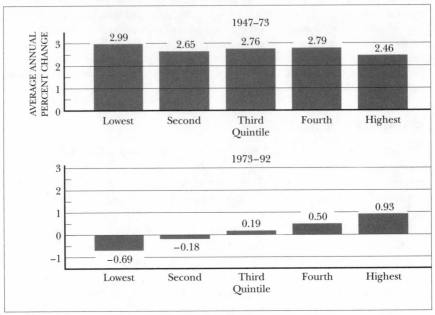

Source: Department of Commerce.

up only slightly, averaging 1.2 percent on an annual basis. [There is a] close relation between productivity and real compensation. Boxes 2 and 3 discuss some of the other effects of productivity growth.

The productivity slowdown has been intensely studied. Many partial explanations have been given, but no complete accounting has been made.

EXPLAINING THE GROWTH OF INEQUALITY

Several factors have contributed to widening inequality. One major factor is increasing returns to education and experience. The college–high school wage premium increased by over 100 percent for workers aged 25 to 34 between 1974 and 1992, while increasing 20 percent for all workers 18 years old and over. In addition, among workers without college degrees, the average wages of older workers increased relative to those of younger workers. Since the relative supply of educated workers has increased at the same time that wage disparities have grown, the demand for educated workers must have increased faster than their supply. Some have suggested

CHART 3   Productivity Growth and Price Reductions, 1950–90

Productivity growth in an industry leads to lower relative prices.

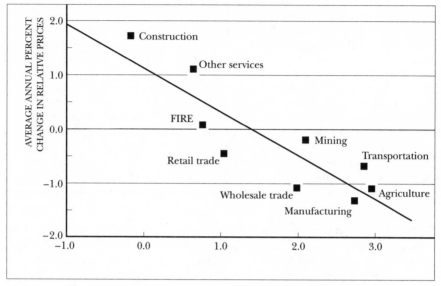

AVERAGE ANNUAL PERCENT CHANGE IN PRODUCTIVITY

Note: FIRE = finance, insurance, and real estate.

Source: Department of Commerce.

BOX 2.   **CONSEQUENCES OF PRODUCTIVITY GROWTH**

Rising productivity has been shown to have a variety of beneficial effects:

■ *The prices of goods produced by industries that have had rapid productivity growth have fallen relative to those of goods from industries with slower productivity growth.* Chart 3 shows average productivity growth and price changes by industry for the 1950–90 period.

■ *Periods of rapid productivity growth have been accompanied by increases in real wages.* The prices of products in industries experiencing productivity growth also decline relative to wages. This decline in product prices means that real wages tend to rise during periods of rapid productivity growth.

■ *Periods of rapid productivity growth have also been periods of low inflation.* Productivity growth allows nominal wages to increase without putting pressure on prices.

■ *Periods of rapid productivity growth have not been associated with large increases in unemployment.* In periods when productivity growth was more rapid, such as the 1960s, unemployment rates have tended to be low. In contrast, periods with slow rates of productivity growth, such as the 1970s, have been periods of relatively high unemployment.

BOX 3.   **WHY PRODUCTIVITY GROWTH DOES NOT CAUSE UNEMPLOYMENT**

Productivity growth need not cause an increase in unemployment because, as productivity rises, more goods can be produced with the same number of workers. This means a cost saving, which must result in either increased profits, increased wages, or lower prices. If profits or wages increase, those benefiting from the increase will increase their spending. If prices fall, consumers' incomes will go further and they will buy more. In any case, the increased spending will lead to the purchase of more goods and services, which will create new jobs offsetting losses from the productivity increase. If the new jobs created are not equal in number to the jobs lost, there will be a tendency for wages to change to equate supply and demand for labor. Nonetheless, in the short run some workers are likely to have to change jobs. As the discussion of the costs of job loss makes clear, this can be a traumatic experience for the established worker.

---

that increasing trade has undermined demand for less-educated workers in the United States, since they are plentiful elsewhere in the world. So far, however, several studies have been unable to discern any substantial impact of trade on wage inequality, however. If increased trade were the cause of growing wage inequality, the relative prices of goods that use highly educated labor would be rising relative to those of goods that use less highly educated labor. But studies have found no evidence of such a change in relative prices. Similarly, if increased trade were responsible for increased wage inequality, the growth of wage differentials would lead firms in all sectors to substitute less-educated labor for more-educated labor. Instead, studies find that virtually all manufacturing industries have increased their relative use of educated labor despite growing wage differentials. Rising wage differentials with greater use of educated labor suggest that demand for skilled labor has been rising broadly in the economy. Thus it appears that most of the demand shift toward highly educated workers must have originated domestically.

Since the use of more-educated labor has increased in all industries, a logical explanation of this trend is technical change. For example, one study shows that people who work with personal computers earn a substantial wage premium over those who do not, and that this can account for half of the increasing gap between the wages of college and high school graduates.

Although changes in labor demand induced by changes in the composition of trade do not appear to explain much of the increase in income inequality, the internationalization of the U.S. economy may affect wages in other ways. For example, the threat of increased import competition or of the relocation of a factory to another country may undermine worker bargaining power or cause a decline in the number of workers employed in unionized firms. At this time, no reliable studies have properly quantified how important such effects have been. In addition, there is no guarantee that the future will resemble the past. Trade could become a more important factor in bringing down the wages of less-educated workers in the future. On the other hand, technical change could move in the direction of economizing on educated labor and making better use of less-educated labor.

In addition to rapidly increasing demand for educated labor, two institutional factors seem to have contributed to rising wage inequality: the decline of unions and the erosion of the minimum wage by inflation. In the early 1970s, 27 percent of the work force were union members. By 1990 that fraction had declined to 16 percent, and it has probably fallen further since. Several studies conclude that this decline can account for about 20 percent of the increase in wage inequality.

In 1970 the minimum wage was 50 percent of the average hourly wage of private production and nonsupervisory workers. By 1992 it had fallen to 40 percent of the average. This erosion of the minimum wage has allowed a substantial fattening of the lower tail of the wage distribution and contributed to increasing wage inequality. The effect of the minimum wage on the distribution of income is less obvious, since it is possible that the decline in the inflation-adjusted minimum wage may have caused an increase in employment of low-wage workers.

Immigration has increased the relative supply of less-educated labor and appears to have contributed to the increasing inequality of income, but the effect has been small. A study of the effects of immigration between 1980 and 1988 found that it explains less than 1 percent of the change in the college–high school wage differential. Although immigration flows were considerably larger in the late 1980s than the early 1980s, this study makes it seem unlikely that immigration could explain more than a few percent of the total change in this differential.

Income Mobility and Economic Opportunity

Chris Frenze

JOINT ECONOMIC COMMITTEE OF CONGRESS: RE-PUBLICAN VIEWS*

G reat attention has been given to changes over time in the average incomes of "quintiles," families or households ranked top to bottom by income and divided into fifths. However, such time-line comparisons between rich and poor ignore a central element of the U.S. economy, which is the extent to which individuals move from one quintile to another. Figures on income mobility are more characteristic of the nature of our fluid society than comparisons of average incomes by quintile, which would only be statistically meaningful if America were a caste society where the people comprising the quintiles remained constant over time.

Unfortunately, while data on average income by quintile has been plentiful, however misleading, data on income mobility has been scarce.

This section, an analysis of data based on income tax returns filed from 1979 through 1988, which were tabulated by the U.S. Department of the Treasury, provides new insights. The Treasury sample consists of 14,351 taxpayers filing returns in all of the above years. This sample tends to understate income mobility to the extent the movement of younger and older filers in and out of the population of taxpayers is missed by the requirement that returns be filed in all years. On the other hand, this understate-

*The 1993 Joint Economic Report, Joint Economic Committee of Congress, April 1, 1993.

ment is at least somewhat offset at the low end of the income scale by the presence of an underclass which does not file tax returns year after year. For our purposes, the bottom quintile consists of those who earn enough income to at least file income tax returns, if not to actually pay taxes.

Earlier studies of income mobility have demonstrated a startling degree of income mobility in as short a period as one year. However, as a January 1992 study noted,[1] additional data over more extended periods were needed to draw more precise conclusions about income mobility over the longer term. This need has now been largely satisfied by the provision of longitudinal panel data from tax return files. However, much more data and research on income dynamics in coming years is needed.

LEVEL OF INCOME MOBILITY BY QUINTILE

The tax return data support the conclusion that the degree of income mobility in American society renders the comparison of quintile income levels over time virtually meaningless. According to the tax data, 85.8 percent of filers in the bottom quintile in 1979 had exited this quintile by 1988. The corresponding mobility rates were 71 percent for the second lowest quintile, 67 percent for the middle quintile, 62.5 percent for the fourth quintile, and 35.3 percent for the top quintile.

Of those in the much discussed top 1 percent, over half, or 52.7 percent, were gone by 1988. These data understate income mobility in the top 1 percent to the extent mortality contributes to mobility and the diffusion of income. Chart 4 displays the income mobility of the various groups.

In all but the top quintile, at least 60 percent of filers exited their 1979 income quintile by 1988, with two-thirds or more exiting in the bottom three quintiles. Though much more stability was observed in the top fifth, over one-third had slipped downward to be replaced by others moving up. Even most of the top 1 percent had exited by 1988, to be replaced by others.

The very high degree of income mobility displayed above shows that the composition of the various quintiles changes greatly over time. A majority of filers have indeed moved to different quintiles between 1979 and 1988. Thus intertemporal comparisons of average wages, earnings, or private incomes of quintiles cannot provide meaningful measures of changes in the income of actual families and persons only temporarily in a given quintile or percentile. Quintiles may be a convenient way of presenting snapshots of income data for a group of people at a certain point in time. Nonethe-

---

[1]JEC/GOP staff study, "Income Mobility and the U.S. Economy: Open Society or Caste System?" released by Congressman Dick Armey, January 1992.

CHART 4 Proportion Moving to Different Quintiles or from Top
Percentile, 1979–88

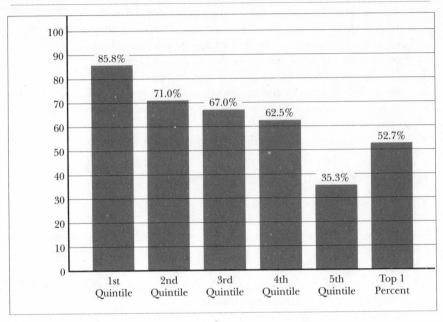

Source: United States Treasury.

less, the notion of a quintile as a fixed economic class or social reality is a
statistical mirage.

DIRECTION OF INCOME MOBILITY

Movement is important, but the direction of that movement is more important. While a strong argument can be made for a flexible and open market economy which presents opportunities to lower and middle income
workers, instability alone is not necessarily a virtue. [Table 1] summarizes
the income mobility data to display the direction of movement between
1979 and 1988. For example, in the third, or middle 1979 fifth, 47.3 percent had moved to a higher quintile by 1988, while 33.0 remained in this
same quintile, and 19.7 percent fell into a lower quintile.

Given the relative starting position, the very high mobility from the bottom quintile obviously reflects improvement. In addition, the upward
movement in the second, third, and fourth quintiles is much larger than

TABLE 1 America on the Move

1979 QUINTILE	PERCENT IN QUINTILE IN 1979	PERCENT IN EACH QUINTILE IN 1988				
		1ST	2ND	3RD	4TH	5TH
1st	100%	14.2%	20.7%	25.0%	25.3%	14.7%
2nd	100	10.9	29.0	29.6	19.5	11.1
3rd	100	5.7	14.0	33.0	32.3	15.0
4th	100	3.1	9.3	14.8	37.5	35.4
5th	100	1.1	4.4	9.4	20.3	64.7

Source: United States Treasury.

downward movement. For example, 60 percent of the second quintile had moved to one of the higher three quintiles by 1988. Over this same time, only 10.9 percent had fallen from the second into the lowest quintile.

In the long-overdue debate over the significance of income mobility, some may argue that mobility would tend to reflect slippage, especially among the middle class. The data contradict this contention. Of those in the middle quintile in 1979, nearly half moved upward to the fourth or fifth quintiles by 1988. Overall, in the bottom four quintiles, net improvement was the rule, not the exception.

DETAIL ON INCOME MOBILITY, 1979–88

Table 1 displays the movement of filers from 1979 quintiles to their positions in 1988. Each row can be read across: of 100 percent of each 1979 quintile, the table shows their dispersion among the various fifths by 1988.

About 86 percent of those in the bottom quintile in 1979 had managed to raise their incomes by 1988 enough to have moved up to a higher quintile. The data show that these were not all grouped at the bottom at the second quintile. While 20.7 percent were in the second quintile, 25.0 percent had made it into the middle fifth, and another 25.3 percent into the second highest quintile. The 14.7 percent in the top quintile was actually higher than the 14.2 percent still stuck in the bottom fifth.

In other words, a member of the bottom income bracket in 1979 would have a better chance of moving to the top income bracket by 1988 than remaining in the bottom bracket.

In the second quintile, 71 percent had exited between 1979 and 1988. Though 29.0 percent still remained in the second quintile in 1988, 29.6

percent had moved up to the third quintile, 19.5 percent to the fourth, and 11.1 percent to the top quintile. Only 10.9 percent had moved down to the lowest quintile.

Of those in the middle quintile in 1979, 32.3 percent had moved to the fourth quintile and 15.0 percent to the fifth quintile by 1988.

Over this period, 47.3 percent had moved up, while 19.7 percent had moved down. The net effect of income mobility in the middle range clearly reflected net overall improvement.

While the fourth quintile exhibited powerful income mobility, the top quintile is the most stable. However, all income mobility from the top quintile is by definition downward mobility. The share of this group dropping into lower quintiles was 35.3 percent, while 27.2 percent of the fourth quintile also dropped at least one quintile. Many of these with declining fortunes are still better off than many of those with upward mobility from a low quintile, however, the overall pattern is that there tends to be strong upward mobility from the lower quintiles, while income mobility from a high level often reflects economic reversals. Without income mobility, many in the top fifth would be better off, and the great majority of those in the lower quintiles would be worse off. Income mobility reflects improvement in the lower four quintiles, but this fact has been virtually ignored in public discussion of income trends.

While 35.3 percent fell from the top quintile into the fourth quintile or below, 40.0 percent of the bottom quintile had moved into the fourth or fifth quintiles by 1988. Of all of those in the bottom quintile in 1979, about two-thirds, or 65 percent, had moved to the middle or higher quintiles by 1988. These data demonstrate that the U.S. economy, not without problems over this period, still remains dynamic, open, and productive enough to permit most Americans in the bottom three-fifths to work their way up the economic ladder. What is needed are policies to ensure that this flexibility and opportunity are extended as widely as possible, especially to those who actually fall below the bottom fifth of taxpayers.

Currently there are two models of the American economy, one static, and the other dynamic. The first portrays the United States as a caste system and misapplies the characteristics of a permanent income strata to those only temporarily moving through income brackets. The alternative view portrays a much more complex and interesting social reality in which the composition of income classes are in constant flux. According to this latter point of view, simplistic generalizations about actual persons and families (or "the rich" and "the poor") cannot be drawn from data on a conceptual artifice that does not exist as such in reality.

The empirical data support the view of the market economy as a dynamic and open society that provides opportunity to those who participate. There is no evidence of stagnation, with the turnover rate in the most stable quintile—the top fifth—exceeding 35 percent. The turnover rates in the bottom four quintiles were at least 60 percent over the period, with most of this reflecting upward progress. Analysis that assumes or suggests stable composition of family or household income quintiles rests on invalid assumptions.

It makes no sense to draw sweeping conclusions such as "the income of the bottom 20 percent of families fell" in a 15-year period when most of the people originally in that category have long since improved their standard of living enough to have moved up from the bracket entirely.

David Card

Alan Kreuger

Effects of the Minimum Wage: Alternative Views

DAVID CARD AND ALAN KREUGER

A Challenge to the Traditional View*

Nearly 50 years ago, George Stigler implored economists to be "outspoken, and singularly agreed" that increases in the minimum wage reduce employment. The reasoning behind this prediction is simple and compelling. According to the model presented in nearly every introductory economics textbook, an increase in the minimum wage lowers the employment of minimum-wage workers. This logic has convinced most economists: polls show that more than 90 percent of professional economists agree with the prediction that a higher minimum wage reduces employment. Such a high degree of consensus is remarkable in a profession renowned for its bitter disagreements. But there is one problem: *the evidence is not singularly agreed that increases in the minimum wage reduce employment.* [We] present a new body of evidence showing that recent minimum-wage increases have not had the negative employment effects predicted by the textbook model. Some of the new evidence points toward a *positive* effect of the minimum wage on employment; most shows no effect at all. Moreover, a reanalysis of previous minimum-wage studies finds little support for the prediction that minimum wages reduce employment. If accepted, our findings call into question the standard model of the labor

*This is an excerpt from David Card and Alan Krueger, *Myth and Measurement* (Princeton: Princeton University Press, 1995). Professors Card and Krueger are at Princeton University.

market that has dominated economists' thinking for the past half century.

Our main empirical findings can be summarized as follows. First, a study of employment in the fast-food industry after the recent 1992 increase in the New Jersey minimum wage shows that employment was *not* affected adversely by the law. Our results are derived from a specially designed survey of more than 400 restaurants throughout New Jersey and eastern Pennsylvania, conducted before and after the increase in the New Jersey minimum wage. Relative to restaurants in Pennsylvania, where the minimum wage remained unchanged, we find that employment in New Jersey actually *expanded* with the increase in the minimum wage. Furthermore, when we examine restaurants within New Jersey, we find that employment growth was *higher* at restaurants that were forced to increase their wages to comply with the law than at those stores that already were paying more than the new minimum. We find similar results in studies of fast-food restaurants in Texas after the 1991 increase in the federal minimum wage, and of teenage workers after the 1988 increase in California's minimum wage.

Second, a cross-state analysis finds that the 1990 and 1991 increases in the federal minimum wage did not affect teenage employment adversely. The federal minimum increased from $3.35 per hour to $3.80 on April 1, 1990, and to $4.25 per hour on April 1, 1991. We categorized states into groups on the basis of the fraction of teenage workers who were earning between $3.35 and $3.80 per hour just before the first minimum-wage increase took effect. In high-wage states, such as California and Massachusetts, relatively few teenagers were in the range in which the minimum-wage increase would affect pay rates, whereas in low-wage states, such as Mississippi and Alabama, as many as 50 percent of teenagers were in the affected wage range. On the basis of the textbook model of the minimum wage, one would expect teenage employment to decrease in the low-wage states, where the federal minimum wage raised pay rates, relative to high-wage states, where the minimum had far less effect. Contrary to this expectation, our results show no meaningful difference in employment growth between high-wage and low-wage states. If anything, the states with the largest fraction of workers affected by the minimum wage had the largest gains in teenage employment. This conclusion continues to hold when we adjust for differences in regional economic growth that occurred during the early 1990s, and conduct the analysis with state-level data, rather than regional data. A similar analysis of employment trends for a broader sample of low-wage workers, and for employees in the retail trade and restaurant industries, likewise fails to uncover a negative employment effect of the federal minimum wage.

Third, we update and reevaluate the time-series analysis of teenage employment that is the most widely cited evidence for the prediction that a higher minimum wage reduces employment. When the same econometric specifications that were used during the 1970s are re-estimated with data from more recent years, the historical relationship between minimum wages and teenage employment is weaker and no longer statistically significant. We also discuss and reanalyze several previous minimum-wage studies that used cross-sectional or panel data. We find that the evidence showing the minimum wage has no effect or a positive effect on employment is at least as compelling as the evidence showing it has an adverse effect.

Fourth, we document a series of anomalies associated with the low-wage labor market and the minimum wage. An increase in the minimum wage leads to a situation in which workers who previously were paid different wages all receive the new minimum wage. This finding is difficult to reconcile with the view that each worker originally was paid exactly what he or she was worth. Increases in the minimum wage also generate a "ripple effect," leading to pay raises for workers who previously earned wages above the new minimum. More surprisingly, increases in the minimum wage do not appear to be offset by reductions in fringe benefits. Furthermore, employers have been reluctant to use the subminimum-wage provisions of recent legislation. Each of these findings casts further doubt on the validity of the textbook model of the minimum wage.

Fifth, we find that recent increases in the minimum wage have reduced wage dispersion, partially reversing the trend toward rising wage inequality that has dominated the labor market since the early 1980s. Contrary to popular stereotypes, minimum-wage increases accrue disproportionately to individuals in low-income families. Indeed, two-thirds of minimum-wage earners are adults, and the earnings of a typical minimum-wage worker account for about one-half of his or her family's total earnings. In states in which the recent increases in the federal minimum wage had the greatest impact on wages, we find that earnings increased for families at the bottom of the earnings distribution. The minimum wage is a blunt instrument for reducing overall poverty, however, because many minimum-wage earners are not in poverty, and because many of those in poverty are not connected to the labor market. We calculate that the 90-cent increase in the minimum wage between 1989 and 1991 transferred roughly $5.5 billion to low-wage workers (or 0.2 percent of economy-wide earnings)—an amount that is smaller than most other federal antipoverty programs, and that can have only limited effects on the overall income distribution.

Sixth, we examine the impact of news about minimum-wage legislation on the value of firms that employ minimum-wage workers. Stock market event studies suggest that most of the news about the impending minimum-wage increases during the late 1980s led to little or no change in the market value of low-wage employers, such as restaurants, hotels, and dry cleaners. In contrast, more recent news of possible increases in the minimum wage may have led to small declines in shareholder wealth—1 or 2 percent, at most.

If a single study found anomalous evidence on the employment effect of the minimum wage, it could be easily dismissed. But the broad array of evidence presented in this book is more difficult to dismiss. Taken as a whole, our findings pose a serious challenge to the simple textbook theory that economists have used to describe the effect of the minimum wage.

Effects of the Minimum Wage: Alternative Views

GARY S. BECKER

It's Simple: Hike the Minimum Wage, and You Put People Out of Work*

Higher labor costs reduce employment. That is why President Clinton's proposal to raise the federal minimum wage should be rejected. A higher minimum will further reduce the employment opportunities of workers with few skills.

Teenagers, high school dropouts, immigrants, and other low-skilled workers frequently earn less than $5.15 per hour, the proposed new minimum. They find employment in small establishments, especially in fast-food chains and other retail sectors. Increasing the minimum, as the President wants, would put some of them out of work since their productivity is not high enough to justify the cost to employers.

During the past several decades, many studies found that raising the minimum wage does reduce the employment of teenagers and others with low skills. But minimum-wage laws have remained popular among trade unionists and many politicians. And periodically, some economists have contested the prevailing wisdom about harmful effects.

*This article appeared in *Business Week*, March 6, 1995. Gary Becker is professor of economics at the University of Chicago.

SERIOUS FLAWS

A recent and widely cited challenge of this kind has come from several studies by two Princeton University economists, David Card and Alan B. Krueger—the latter now Robert B. Reich's chief economist at the Labor Department. One study finds that the change in employment after a minimum-wage hike is generally not bigger in states with a larger fraction of low-wage workers—the group that should be most affected by higher minimums.

Another study is frequently mentioned by Reich and others in the Administration to bolster the argument that a higher minimum does not lower employment. That study compares employment changes in fast-food restaurants in New Jersey and Pennsylvania after New Jersey raised its own minimum in 1992. Card and Krueger argue that because employment fell in Pennsylvania as much as it did in New Jersey, the drop in both states must have been due to other causes than the raise in the minimum.

There are some, and I am one of them, who believe that these studies have serious defects. Several of these were spelled out by Donald R. Deere and Finis R. Welch of Texas A&M University and Kevin M. Murphy of the University of Chicago in research they reported at the January meetings of the American Economic Association.

For example, the higher federal minimum in 1990 and 1991 caused a much larger drop in New Jersey's teenage employment than Pennsylvania's, which could explain why employment did not fall more in New Jersey when that state increased its own minimum in 1992. New Jersey employers presumably anticipated the increase in their state's minimum when they sharply cut employment in responding to the earlier wage hike.

DUELING STUDIES

The Card-Krueger studies are flawed and cannot justify going against the accumulated evidence from the many past and present studies that find sizable negative effects of higher minimums on employment. The Deere, Murphy, and Welch study shows that the two-stepped increase in the federal minimum from $3.35 to $4.25 in 1990 and 1991 reduced employment of teenagers, high school dropouts, and other groups with low earnings.

The magnitude of these reductions sounds about right, particularly after the authors take into account the economic recession of that time. After the 27% increase in the minimum wage, employment of male and female teenagers lowered by 12% and 18%, respectively, while employment of high school dropouts shrank by about 6%. If Congress raises the rate by 18%, to $5.15 an hour, these results imply that employment of workers with few skills will fall by over 5%.

President Clinton justified the need for a higher rate of pay by noting that a family cannot live decently on minimum-wage earnings. However, even Card and Krueger do not find that raising the minimum is an effective way to reduce poverty, since poor families typically get only a small fraction of their income from members whose wages are near the minimum.

The President also wants to increase current subsidization of the job training of less skilled workers, but these subsidies might be unnecessary if Clinton did not also advocate raising federal minimum wages. Higher minimums discourage on-the-job training of workers with few skills since they spend their time learning rather than producing.

Even a wizard would have a great deal of difficulty repealing the economic law that higher minimum wages reduce employment. Since politicians are not wizards, they should not try.

QUESTIONS FOR ANALYSIS

1. What are the effects of productivity growth? Does productivity growth have to cause unemployment? Why or why not?

2. Are there any reasons why we should be concerned about increases or decreases in income inequality? If so, what are they?

3. According to President Clinton's Council of Economic Advisers, "Stagnant wages and slow total compensation growth since the early 1970s largely reflect a substantial slowdown in productivity growth." Why would a slowdown in productivity growth be expected to have this effect? Explain.

4. President Clinton's Council of Economic Advisers concludes that: "Rising wage differentials with greater use of educated labor suggest that demand for skilled labor has been rising broadly in the economy." Can you show that this is the case, using demand and supply curves for educated labor?

5. Other factors cited by President Clinton's Council of Economic Advisers as possible reasons for growing wage inequality are "the decline of unions and the erosion of the minimum wage by inflation." Are increases in *wage* inequality the same thing as increases in *income* inequality? Why or why not? Is it possible that a big hike in the minimum wage might raise, not lower, income inequality? Why or why not?

6. According to the Republican members of Congress's Joint Economic Committee, "Great attention has been given to changes over time in the average incomes of 'quintiles,' families or households ranked top to bottom by income and divided into fifths. However, such time-line comparisons between rich and poor ignore a central element of the U.S. economy, which is the extent to which individuals move from one quintile to another." Do you agree that such movement is important? Why or why not?

7. The Republican members of the Joint Economic Committee state that: "The empirical data support the view of the market economy as a dynamic and open society that provides opportunity to those who participate." Do you agree? Why or why not?

8. Do you agree with the following conclusion: "It makes no sense to draw sweeping conclusions such as 'the income of the bottom 20 percent of families fell' in a 15-year period when most of the people originally in that category have long since improved their standard of living enough to have moved up from the bracket entirely." Why do you agree or disagree?

9. According to Stanford's Paul Krugman, "the median individual who moved from the bottom to the top 20 percent was only 22 years old at the beginning of the study period."* Does this matter? Why or why not?

10. According to Professors Card and Krueger, their findings "pose a serious challenge to the simple textbook theory that economists have used to describe the effect of the minimum wage." Why?

11. Professor Becker maintains that the "Card-Krueger studies are flawed and cannot justify going against the accumulated evidence from the many past and present studies that find sizable negative effects of higher minimums on employment." Why does he believe that President Clinton's proposal to raise the minimum wage should be rejected? Do you agree? Why or why not?

*New York Times, August 21, 1995, p. A15

PART TWO

WELFARE

REFORM

One of the most controversial issues in the United States is welfare reform. There is considerable agreement that the current welfare system has major flaws, but much less agreement over what should be done to improve it. The first article, the highly publicized *Contract with America* by the Republican members of the U.S. House of Representatives, says that spending for welfare programs should be reduced and welfare limited to two years. The second article, by Senator Daniel Patrick Moynihan (D., NY), argues that destitution in childhood, relatively independent of economic forces, has become our principal social problem. The third article, by President Clinton's Council of Economic Advisers, emphasizes the importance of raising the rewards and hence the incentives for the poor to work.

Contract with America

**REPUBLICAN MEMBERS OF THE U.S. HOUSE OF REPRE-
SENTATIVES***

Within the first 100 days of the 104th Congress, we shall bring to the House Floor the following bills, each to be given full and open debate, each to be given a clear and fair vote and each to be immediately available this day for public inspection and scrutiny.

1. The Fiscal Responsibility Act
A balanced budget/tax limitation amendment and a legislative line-item veto to restore fiscal responsibility to an out-of-control Congress, requiring them to live under the same budget constraints as families and businesses.

2. The Taking Back Our Streets Act
An anti-crime package including stronger truth-in-sentencing, "good faith" exclusionary rule exemptions, effective death penalty provisions, and cuts in social spending from this summer's "crime" bill to fund prison construction and additional law enforcement to keep people secure in their neighborhoods and kids safe in their schools.

3. The Personal Responsibility Act
Discourage illegitimacy and teen pregnancy by prohibiting welfare to

*This is an excerpt from the *Contract with America,* put forth by the Republican Members of the U.S. House of Representatives.

minor mothers and denying increased AFDC (Aid to Families with Dependent Children) for additional children while on welfare, cut spending for welfare programs, and enact a tough two-years-and-out provision with work requirements to promote individual responsibility.

4. The Family Reinforcement Act
Child support enforcement, tax incentives for adoption, strengthening rights of parents in their children's education, stronger child pornography laws, and an elderly dependent care tax credit to reinforce the central role of families in American society.

5. The American Dream Restoration Act
A $500 per child tax credit, begin repeal of the marriage tax penalty, and creation of American Dream Savings Accounts to provide middle class tax relief.

6. The National Security Restoration Act
No U.S. troops under U.N. command and restoration of the essential parts of our national security funding to strengthen our national defense and maintain our credibility around the world.

7. The Senior Citizens Fairness Act
Raise the Social Security earnings limit which currently forces seniors out of the work force, repeal the 1993 tax hikes on Social Security benefits and provide tax incentives for private long-term care insurance to let Older Americans keep more of what they have earned over the years.

8. The Job Creation and Wage Enhancement Act
Small business incentives, capital gains cut and indexation, neutral cost recovery, risk assessment/cost-benefit analysis, strengthening the Regulatory Flexibility Act and unfunded mandate reform to create jobs and raise worker wages.

9. The Common Sense Legal Reform Act
"Loser pays" laws, reasonable limits on punitive damages and reform of product liability laws to stem the endless tide of litigation.

10. The Citizen Legislature Act
A first-ever vote on term limits to replace career politicians with citizen legislators. . . .

Dependency Is Our New Problem

DANIEL PATRICK MOYNIHAN*

In 1965, I published the first data that suggested that we might be moving into an era in which destitution in childhood, relatively independent of economic forces, would be our principal social problem. This was, I believe, a new proposition.

It dealt with dependency, the growing number of children born to single parents and dependent during childhood on what Pope John Paul II calls "the social assistance state." The U.S. Department of Labor came upon indications that the connection between child welfare and the workplace was breaking up. Earlier, when unemployment had dropped, new welfare cases dropped. No longer. Seemingly, dependency was an independent variable, possibly out of control.

This seemed especially so among minorities, a proposition I took to President Lyndon B. Johnson, who said as much in an address at Howard University in 1965. The president's analysis, however, was rejected. People said it wasn't so, and we could not prove otherwise. In truth, nothing much had yet happened. We had these indicators, but no more. And so we had to wait for the answer, or at least an approximate answer. We now have it. We were right.

*This article appeared in *Newsday,* October 18, 1991. Daniel Patrick Moynihan is New York's senior U.S. senator.

Specifically, we now know that of children born in the years 1967–69, some 22.1 percent were dependent on welfare (Aid to Families with Dependent Children, or AFDC) before reaching age 18. This breaks down to 15.7 percent for white children, 72.3 percent for black children.

What about the cohorts that followed? We don't finally know, but we can make an educated guess. The data tell us that children under the age of 8 were, on average, 36.8 percent more likely to have been on AFDC in the 1970s than their predecessors in the 1960s. If we assume that this same increase will show up for the whole of the 18 years (0–17), then we can project rates for children born as late as 1980. This gives us a white rate of 22.2 percent, and a black rate of 82.9 percent. (The latter would seem too high, and is, of course, only a projection. Still, we face the daunting possibility that five in six minority children are destitute and on welfare by age 18.)

This surely raises the issue of social justice—if, that is, it can be shown that such destitution in childhood is, in the main, a debilitating event. Not for each individual, but generally speaking for a class of individuals. Lawrence M. Mead of New York University believes this to be so. In "The New Dependency Politics" he writes: "The inequalities that stem from the workplace are now trivial in comparison to those stemming from family structure. What matters for success is not whether your father was rich or poor but whether you had a father at all."

This question has to be addressed: *Has* a new social condition appeared? Is something new going on? Are we missing something large? As an example, in February, 1991, some months before the report of the National Commission on Children appeared, the Senate Democratic Caucus had approved a legislative program entitled, "Strengthening America: The Democratic Agenda." A section on children included this passage: "There are some 64 million children in the United States. At current dependency rates, 16 million, or one-quarter, will be on welfare before they have reached the age of 18. . . . Children now make up the largest proportion of poor persons in the United States. There is no equivalent in our history to such a number or such a proportion.

"All this is new. This circumstance did not exist during the era of the New Deal, a half century ago. It did not exist during the era of the Great Society, a quarter century ago. It marks the emergence of a new issue in social policy. The issue of dependency."

However, before the document was sent to the printer, an "error" was spotted by the committee staff. The text that read: "This circumstance did not exist during the era of the New Deal, a half century ago. It did not exist during the era of the Great Society, a quarter century ago," was changed to read: "This circumstance was *not as recognized* during the era of the New Deal, a half century ago, nor during the era of the Great Society, a quarter century ago" (emphasis added).

As I had written that passage, I asked about the change. It became transparently clear that those responsible had simply thought they were correcting a mistake. This is becoming the liberal orthodoxy: that there is nothing new. It is not, come to think, so very different from the views of those in the nineteenth Century who, on observing an industrial society all around them, could not conceive that society had changed to the extent that institutions needed to change as well. Thorstein Veblen called it "cultural lag."

My 1965 article [in the magazine *America*] began: "The United States is very possibly on the verge of adopting a national policy directed to the quality and stability of American family life." In this I was quite wrong. We did nothing of the sort. The evidence was rejected as inconclusive or worse. It is still rejected in the sense that orthodox opinion rejects the notion that there is anything qualitatively different about the present, insisting instead that the federal government simply do more of what we have been doing.

James S. Coleman of the University of Chicago traces our present situation back to the emergence of the corporation in medieval Europe and its gradual displacement of kinship structures. Is it possible that some general theory will come along that will tease out the sources of welfare dependency and get this problem back down to an acceptable level as Keynes did with unemployment? A reassuring thought, actually.

That would be for the long run. For purposes of the short run, it may be useful to note that in 1988 Congress enacted the Family Support Act, the first change in the welfare system since it was established as a federal program in the midst of that Great Depression. In recent Senate testimony, Judith Gueron, president of the Manpower Demonstration Research Corp., described the legislation: "The vision of welfare reform that we see reflected in the FSA [Family Support Act] is of a 'social contract' between poor parents and government, in which each party has responsibilities. Parents—both mothers and fathers—have the responsibility to contribute to the support of their children to the best of their abilities and to engage in activities designed to improve their self-sufficiency. The responsibilities of government are to provide the means for poor parents to become self-sufficient—such as employment services and supports—and to provide income when their best efforts fall short."

It remains to be seen whether the Family Support Act will be made to work. It is, in any event, only one of many measures that will be called for if, as is at the very least likely, the issue of dependency becomes the central issue of social justice in the next century. Come to think, millennium.

Welfare Reform

PRESIDENT CLINTON'S COUNCIL OF ECONOMIC AD-VISERS*

President [Clinton] entered office with a promise to reform the welfare system so that it would function as an effective safety net promoting work and family, rather than as a snare enmeshing poor families in long-term dependence. Under the current system some people have become long-term welfare recipients—although more than one-third of all women who ever receive Aid to Families with Dependent Children [AFDC] do so for less than 2 years, almost one-fourth end up receiving [it] for over 10 years during their lifetime. And, as currently structured, the welfare system in effect imposes a high marginal tax rate on paid employment, because low-income mothers lose their AFDC and food stamp benefits and eventually their Medicaid health insurance for themselves and their children when they take a job. In short, for many the current system contains powerful disincentives against work and in favor of continued welfare.

The fundamental goal of all of the Administration's policies aimed at those at the lower end of the income distribution is to increase the rewards and hence the incentives to work. These policies are also designed to ensure that those willing to work will be able to live above the poverty level

*This article is an excerpt from the *Economic Report of the President* (Washington, D.C.: Government Printing Office, 1995).

BOX 4   **HUD REFORMS AND WELFARE REFORM**

The Administration has proposed major reforms aimed at reinventing the Federal Government's housing programs. These reforms will focus the efforts of the Department of Housing and Urban Development (HUD) on two major tasks: empowering individuals and empowering communities.

The Administration's proposals for empowering individuals in the housing market bear a close connection to its proposals to reform welfare. The HUD reforms will gradually end public housing as we know it, moving from support of public housing *projects* to support of individuals who need housing. The current system impedes the job mobility of public housing recipients. In order to accept a job in another community, a recipient may have to give up the subsidized public housing he or she has and sign up at the bottom of a waiting list for housing assistance in the new location. In addition, public housing often concentrates the poor in areas where few jobs are available close at hand. Under the reinvention proposal, instead of being tied to a particular unit in a public housing project, households would be given portable rental housing certificates, which could be used to obtain housing in the private market. This reform would encourage mobility between jobs, impose market discipline on public housing authorities, help break up the dysfunctional concentration of the poor, and enable individuals to make housing choices best suited to their needs. In all these ways the HUD reform effort complements welfare reform by removing barriers to participation in the paid labor force.

(see Box 4 for a discussion of how housing reforms relate to welfare reform).

The Administration's proposed welfare reform legislation, the Work and Responsibility Act, will help make work pay, by ensuring that welfare recipients obtain the skills they need to find employment, and by eliminating long-term welfare dependency as an option for those able to work. Under the Administration's plan, welfare recipients who are job-ready will begin a job search immediately, and anyone offered a job will be required to take it. Support for child care will be provided to help people move from dependence to independence. For those not ready for work, the administration's proposed reforms will provide support, job training, and assistance in finding a job when they are ready. Each adult recipient of AFDC will be required to create an employability plan, to ensure that he or she will move into the work force as quickly as possible. Time limits on receipt of welfare benefits will require that anyone who can work, must work—in the private sector if possible, in a temporary, subsidized job if necessary.

The proposed program will strongly discourage children from bearing children. Parents under the age of 18, if they apply for welfare payments, generally will not be allowed to set up independent households; instead they will receive assistance to stay in school. The Administration's proposal also includes funding for grants to schools and communities to prevent teen pregnancy, and it toughens efforts to collect child support from all absent fathers—a provision that is expected to double Federal collections of child support payments, from $9 billion to an estimated $20 billion by 2000. These proposals to discourage teen pregnancy and to foster parental responsibility will help prevent the need for welfare in the first place.

In welfare as in other areas of joint Federal and State responsibility to help the poor, such as Medicaid, the Administration is committed to working with the States to enhance the flexibility and efficiency of programs. For this reason the Administration has been an active proponent of granting waivers from various regulatory constraints, to allow states to experiment with new ways of designing welfare strategies and find the ones that

---

BOX 5   EMPOWERMENT ZONES AND ENTERPRISE COMMUNITIES

The empowerment zone/enterprise community program is based on the notion that development efforts can be targeted to areas that have been economically left behind. Besides receiving monetary awards totalling $1.3 billion in financial assistance and $2.5 billion in tax benefits over the next 5 years, the selected zones and communities (as well as nonselected applicants) may request waivers from many Federal regulations, and their requests will be processed on an expedited basis. To date over 1,200 such requests have been received. Perhaps more important, the areas selected generally are those that have effectively mobilized local private and public sector resources to leverage the potential Federal commitments. The application process encouraged localities to harness their own creative talents and financial resources to frame a comprehensive response to the problems of local economic development.

In a sense, the zones and communities selected are laboratories for experiments in local economic development. The Federal Government realizes that it does not have all the answers to the economic development conundrum; instead it has enlisted institutions at the State and the local level (including the private and nonprofit sectors) to help design possible solutions.

For the program to work, however, successful areas and the reasons for their success must be identified. Therefore a comprehensive evaluation process will follow the progress of the selected zones and communities and report periodically on them. The evaluation will largely determine whether the program should be replicated elsewhere.

best suit their particular needs and characteristics. During its first 2 years in office, this Administration granted waivers to enable 24 States to undertake welfare reform—more than all previous Administrations combined.

Partnerships with State and local governments take many forms. Box 5 describes one of the Administration's initiatives for working with State and local governments to encourage community-based solutions to economic development problems in poverty-stricken areas.

QUESTIONS FOR ANALYSIS

1. According to the *Contract with America,* the prohibition of welfare payments to minor mothers and the denial of increased public aid for additional children while on welfare would discourage illegitimacy and teen pregnancy. Do you agree? Why or why not?

2. The *Contract with America* also calls for "a tough two-years-and-out provision with work requirements." What would happen if, after a welfare recipient received payments for the maximum period of time, he or she could not find a job?

3. Senator Moynihan emphasizes that children now make up the largest proportion of poor persons in the United States. Why is he concerned about this fact?

4. Moynihan quotes with approval the following statement by Lawrence Mead: "The inequalities that stem from the workplace are now trivial in comparison to those stemming from family structure. What matters for success is not whether your father was rich or poor but whether you had a father at all." Do you agree? Why or why not?

5. What can the government do to influence family structure? What, if any, measures would you favor? Why?

6. President Clinton's Council of Economic Advisers calls attention to the disincentives against work and in favor of continued welfare in the current system. What are these disincentives?

7. Many welfare recipients have very limited education and few job skills. The Clinton Administration's proposed welfare reform legislation "will help make work pay, by ensuring that welfare recipients obtain the skills they need to find employment . . ." Will this be easy? Will it be cheap?

8. According to the proposed welfare reform legislation, "Time limits on receipt of welfare benefits will require that anyone who can work, must work—in the private sector if possible, in a temporary, subsidized job if necessary." Are the necessary subsidies likely to be large? Are the subsidized jobs likely to be real ones, or are they likely to be camouflaged leisure?

9. According to Nobel laureate Friedrich von Hayek, a leading conservative economist, "All societies have unequal wealth and income dispersion, and there is no positive basis for criticizing any degree of market determined inequality." Do you agree? Why or why not?

10. Robert Reich, Secretary of Labor, has said, "The moral core at the heart of capitalism, the faith that if you work hard you can get ahead, is being eroded."* Do you agree? Why or why not? If you do agree, what difference does it make— and what can be done about it?

New York Times, June 4, 1995, p. 4E.

PART THREE

COMPETITION

ON THE

INFORMATION

SUPERHIGH-

WAY

Fundamental changes are taking place in the telecommunications industry. Technological change is making competition feasible in areas where it formerly was not considered possible. The first article, by Vice President Al Gore, describes the Clinton administration's policies with regard to this important and fast-moving area. The second article, by President Bush's Council of Economic Advisers, presents the previous administration's views.

The National Information Infrastructure

AL GORE*

I t's great to be here at the Television Academy today. I feel I have a lot in common with those of you who are members of the Academy. I was on Letterman. I wrote my own lines.

I'm still waiting for residuals.

At first, I thought this could lead to a whole new image. And maybe a new career. No more Leno jokes about being stiffer than the Secret Service. Maybe an opportunity to do other shows. I was elated when "Star Trek: The Next Generation" wanted me to do a guest shot—until I learned they wanted me to replace Lieutenant Commander Data.

The historian Daniel Boorstin once wrote that for Americans "nothing has happened unless it is on television." This of course leaves out a few major events in our history. But this meeting today is on television—so apparently this event is actually occurring.

I join you to outline not only this Administration's vision of the National Information Infrastructure but our proposals for creating it.

Last month in Washington, I set forth some of the principles behind our vision. Today I'll talk about the legislative package necessary to ensure the creation of that national infrastructure in a manner which will connect and

*Al Gore is Vice President of the United States. This speech was delivered before the Television Academy, at the University of California at Los Angeles, on January 11, 1994.

empower the citizens of this country through broadband, interactive communication.

We've all become used to stumbling over cliches in our efforts to describe the enormity of change now underway and the incredible speed with which it is taking place. Often we call it a revolution—the digital revolution.

Speaking of cliches, I often use the analogy to autos, saying that if cars had advanced as rapidly as computer chips in recent years, a Rolls Royce would go a million miles an hour and cost twenty-five cents.

The last time I used it was at a meeting of computer experts and one of them said, "Yeah—but that Rolls Royce would be one millimeter long."

What we've seen in the last decade is amazing. But it's nothing compared to what will happen in the decade ahead. The word revolution by no means overstates the case.

But this revolution is based on traditions that go far back in our history.

Since the transcontinental telegraph that transmitted Abraham Lincoln's election victory to California in real time, our ability to communicate electronically has informed and shaped America.

It was only a year before that election that the Pony Express was the talk of the nation, able to send a message cross country in seven days. The next year, it was out of business.

Today's technology has made possible a global community united by instantaneous information and analysis. Protestors at the Berlin Wall communicated with their followers through CNN news broadcasts. The fax machine connected us with demonstrators at Tiananmen Square.

So it's worth remembering that while we talk about this digital revolution as if it's about to happen, in many places it's already underway. Even in the White House.

The day after Inauguration, I was astonished to see how relatively primitive the White House communications system was. President Clinton and I took a tour and found operators actually having to pull cords for each call and plug them into jacks. It reminded me of the switchboard used by Ernestine, the Lily Tomlin character.

And there were actually phones like these all over the White House. They're still there. But we made progress. They're only in the press room now.

Those phones didn't meet our needs. So now, especially on trips, I use a cellular phone.

Our new ways of communicating will entertain as well as inform. More importantly, they will educate, promote democracy, and save lives. And in the process they will also create a lot of new jobs. In fact, they're already doing it.

The impact on America's businesses will not be limited just to those who are in the information business either. Virtually every business will find it possible to use these new tools to become more competitive. And by taking the lead in quickly employing these new information technologies, America's businesses will gain enormous advantages in the worldwide marketplace. And that is important because if America is to prosper, we must be able to manufacture goods within our borders and sell them not just in Tennessee but Tokyo—not just in Los Angeles but Latin America.

Last month, when I was in Central Asia, the President of Kyrgyzstan told me his eight-year-old son came to him and said, "Father, I have to learn English."

"But why?" President Akayev asked.

"Because, father, the computer speaks English."

By now, we are becoming familiar with the ability of the new communications technologies to transcend international boundaries and bring our world closer together. But many of you are now in the process of transcending other old boundaries—the boundary lines which have long defined different sectors of the information industry. The speed with which these boundaries are eroding is quite dramatic.

I'm reminded of an idea of Stephen Hawking, the British physicist. Hawking has Lou Gehrig's disease. But thanks to information technology he can still communicate not only to his students and colleagues but to millions around the world. Incidentally, I read the other day that his voice box has an American accent—because it was developed here in California.

Anyway, in that American accent, Hawking has speculated about a distant future when the universe stops expanding and begins to contract. Eventually, all matter comes colliding together in a "Big Crunch," which scientists say could then be followed by another "Big Bang"—a universe expanding outward once again.

Our current information industries—cable, local telephone, long distance telephone, television, film, computers, and others—seem headed for a Big Crunch/Big Bang of their own. The space between these diverse functions is rapidly shrinking—between computers and televisions, for example, or interactive communications and video.

But after the next Big Bang, in the ensuing expansion of the information business, the new marketplace will no longer be divided along current sectoral lines. There may not be cable companies or phone companies or computer companies, as such. Everyone will be in the *bit* business. The *functions* provided will define the marketplace. There will be information conduits, information providers, information appliances and information consumers.

That's the future. It's easy to see where we need to go. It's hard to see how to get there. When faced with the enormity and complexity of the transition some retreat to the view best enunciated by Yogi Berra when he said:

"What we have here is an insurmountable opportunity."

Not long ago this transition did indeed seem too formidable to contemplate, but no longer. Because a remarkable consensus has emerged throughout our country—in business, in public interest groups and in government. This consensus begins with agreement on the right, specific questions we must answer together.

How can government ensure that the information marketplace emerging on the other side of the Big Crunch will permit everyone to be able to compete with everyone else for the opportunity to provide any service to all willing customers? How can we ensure that this new marketplace reaches the entire nation? How can we ensure that it fulfills the enormous promise of education, economic growth and job creation?

Today I will provide the Administration's answers to those questions. But before I do let me state my firm belief that legislative and regulatory action alone will not get us where we need to be. This Administration argued in our National Performance Review last year, that government often acts best when it sets clear goals, acts as a catalyst for the national teamwork required to achieve them, then lets the private and non-profit sector move the ball downfield.

It was in this spirit that then-Governor Clinton and I, campaigning for the White House in 1992, set as a vital national goal linking every classroom in every school in the United States to the National Information Infrastructure.

It was in this same spirit that less than a month ago, I pointed out that when it comes to telecommunications services, schools are the most impoverished institutions in society.

And so I was pleased to hear that some companies participating in the communications revolution are now talking about voluntarily linking every classroom in their service areas to the NII.

Let me be clear. I challenge you, the people in this room, to connect all of our classrooms, all of our libraries, and all of our hospitals and clinics by the year 2000. We must do this to realize the full potential of information to educate, to save lives, provide access to health care and lower medical costs.

Our nation can and must meet this challenge. The best way to do so is by working together. Just as communications industries are moving to the unified information marketplace of the future, so must we move from the traditional adversarial relationship between business and government to a more productive relationship based on consensus. We must build a new model of public-private cooperation that, if properly pursued, can obviate many governmental mandates.

But make no mistake about it—one way or another, we will meet this goal.

As I announced last month, we will soon introduce a legislative package that aggressively confronts the most pressing telecommunications issues, and is based on five principles.

This Administration will:

☐ encourage private investment

☐ provide and protect competition

☐ provide open access to the network

☐ take action to avoid creating a society of information "haves" and "have nots"

☐ encourage flexible and responsive governmental action.

Many of you have our White Paper today, outlining the bill in detail. If you didn't get your copy, it's available on the Internet, right now.

Let me run through the highlights with you—and talk about how they grow out of our five principles.

We begin with two of our basic principles—the need for *private investment* and *fair competition*. The nation needs private investment to complete the construction of the National Information Infrastructure. And competition is the single most critical means of encouraging that private investment.

I referred earlier to the use of the telegraph in 1860, linking the nation together. Congress funded Samuel Morse's first demonstration of the telegraph in 1844. Morse then suggested that a national system be built with federal funding. But Congress said no, that private investment should build the information infrastructure. And that's what happened—to the great and continuing competitive advantage of this country.

Today we must choose competition again and protect it against both suffocating regulation on the one hand and unfettered monopolies on the other.

To understand why competition is so important, let's recall what has happened since the breakup of AT&T ten years ago this month.

As recently as 1987, AT&T was still projecting that it would take until the year 2010 to convert 95 percent of its long distance network to digital technology.

Then it became pressed by the competition. The result? AT&T made its network virtually 100 percent digital by the end of 1991. Meanwhile, over the last decade the price of interstate long distance service for the average residential customer declined over 50 percent.

Now it is time to take the next step. We must open the local telephone exchanges, those wires and switches that link homes and offices to the local telephone companies.

The pressure of competition will be great—and it will drive continuing advancements in technology, quality and cost. One businessman told me recently that he was accelerating his investment in new technology to avoid ending up as "roadkill" on the information superhighway.

To take one example of what competition means, cable companies, long distance companies, and electric utilities must be free to offer two-way communications and local telephone service. To accomplish this goal, our legislative package will establish a federal standard that permits entry to the local telephone markets. Moreover, the FCC will be authorized to reduce regulation for telecommunications carriers that lack market power.

We expect open competition to bring lower prices and better services. But let me be clear: We insist upon safeguards to ensure that new corporate freedoms will not be translated into sudden and unjustified rate increases for telephone consumers.

The advancement of competition will necessarily require more opportunity, as well, for the Regional Bell Operating Companies. Current restrictions on their operations are themselves the legacy of the break-up of AT&T and must be re-examined.

This Administration endorses the basic principles of the Brooks-Dingell bill, which proposes a framework for allowing long-distance and local telephone companies to compete against each other.

Regulation and review of this framework should be transferred from the courts to the Department of Justice and the Federal Communications Commission.

This process of change must be carefully calibrated. We must make sure that Regional Bells will not be able to use their present monopoly positions as unfair leverage into new lines of business. That is why the Administration supports the approach of the Brooks-Dingell provision that requires the approval of the Department of Justice and the Federal Communications Commission before the Regional Bells may provide interexchange services—most notably long distance.

In working with Congress, the Administration will explore the creation of incentives for the Regional Bells. We want to increase the transparency of those facility-based local services that raise concerns associated with cross-subsidization and abuses of monopoly power.

Our view of the entry of local telephone companies into cable television also balances the advantages of competition against the possibility of competitive abuse. We will continue to bar the acquisition of existing cable companies by telephone companies within their local service areas. We need this limitation to ensure that no single giant entity controls access to homes and offices. But to increase diversity and benefit consumers, we will permit telephone companies to provide video programming over new, open access systems.

Even these measures, however, may not eliminate all scarcity in the local loop—those information byways that provide the last electronic connection with homes and offices. For some time, in many places, there are likely to be only one or two broadband, interactive wires, probably owned by cable or telephone companies. In the long run, the local loop may contain a wider set of competitors offering a broad range of interactive services, including wireless, microwave and direct broadcast satellite.

But, for now, we cannot assume that competition in the local loop will end all of the accrued market power of past regulatory advantage and market domination.

We cannot permit the creation of information bottlenecks that adversely affect information providers who use the highways as a means of supplying their customers.

Nor can we permit bottlenecks for information consumers who desire programming that may not be available through the wires that enter their homes or offices.

Preserving the free flow of information requires *open access,* our third basic principle.

How can you sell your ideas, your information, your programs, if an intermediary who is also your competitor has the means to unfairly block your access to customers? We can't subject the free flow of content to artificial constraints at the hands of either government regulators or would-be monopolists.

We must also guard against unreasonable technical obstacles. We know how to do this; we've seen this problem in our past. For example, when railroad tracks were different sizes, a passenger could not travel easily from a town served by one railroad to a town served by another. But the use of standardized tracks permitted the creation of a national system of rail transport.

Accordingly, our legislative package will contain provisions designed to ensure that each telephone carrier's networks will be readily accessible to other users. We will create an affirmative obligation to interconnect and to afford nondiscriminatory access to network facilities, services, functions and information. We must also explore the future of non-commercial broadcasting; there must be public access to the information superhighway.

These measures will preserve the future within the context of our present regulatory structures. But that is not enough. We must move towards a regulatory approach that encourages investment, promotes competition and secures open access. And one that is not just a patchwork quilt of old approaches, but an approach necessary to promote fair competition in the future.

We begin with a simple idea: Similar entities must be treated similarly. But let's be clear: our quest for equal treatment of competing entities will not blind us to the economic realities of the new information marketplace, where apparent similarities may mask important differences.

This idea is best expressed in the story about the man who went into a restaurant and ordered the rabbit stew.

It came, he took a few bites, then called the manager over. "This doesn't taste like rabbit stew!" he said. "It tastes . . . well, it tastes like *horsemeat!*"

The manager was embarrassed. "I actually ran out of rabbit this morning and I—well, I put some horsemeat in."

"How much horsemeat?"

"Well—it's equally divided."

"What's that mean?"

"One horse, one rabbit."

The lesson is obvious. A start-up telephone company isn't the same as a Baby Bell.

What we favor is genuine regulatory symmetry. That means regulation must be based on the services that are offered and the ability to compete— and not on corporate identity, regulatory history or technological process.

For example, our legislative package will grant the Federal Communications Commission the future authority, under appropriate conditions, to impose non-discriminatory access requirements on cable companies. As cable and telephone service become harder and harder to distinguish, this provision will help to ensure that labels derived from past regulatory structures are not translated into inadvertent, unfair competitive advantages.

As different services are grouped within a single corporate structure, we must ensure that these new, combined entities are not caught in a cross-fire of conflicting and duplicative regulatory burdens and standards. This Administration will not let existing regulatory structures impede or distort the evolution of the communications industry.

In the information marketplace of the future, we will obtain our goals of investment, competition and open access only if regulation matches the marketplace. That requires a flexible, adaptable regulatory regime that *encourages* the widespread provision of broadband, interactive digital services.

That is why the Administration proposes the creation of an alternative regulatory regime that is unified, as well as symmetrical. Our new regime would not be mandatory, but it would be available to providers of broadband, interactive services. Such companies could elect to be regulated under the current provisions of the Communications Act or under a new title, Title VII, that would harmonize those provisions in order to provide a single system of regulation. These "Title VII" companies would be able to avoid the danger of conflicting or duplicative regulatory burdens. But in return, they would provide their services and access to their facilities to others on a nondiscriminatory basis. The nation would thus be assured that these companies would provide open access to information providers and consumers and the benefits of competition, including lower prices and higher-quality services, to their customers.

This new method itself illustrates one of our five principles—that *government itself must be flexible.* Our proposals for symmetrical, and ultimately unified, regulation demonstrate how we will initiate governmental action that furthers our substantive principles but that adapts, and disappears, as the need for governmental intervention changes—or ends. They demonstrate, as well, the new relationship of which I spoke earlier—the private and public sectors working together to fulfill our common goals.

The principles that I have described thus far will build an open and free information marketplace. They will lower prices, stimulate demand and expand access to the National Information Infrastructure.

They will, in other words, help to attain our final basic principle—avoiding a society of information "haves" separate from a society of information "have nots."

There was a *Washington Post* headline last month:

"Will the 'Information Superhighway' Detour the Poor?"

Not if I have anything to do about it. After all, governmental action to ensure universal service has been part of American history since the days of Ben Franklin's Post Office. We will have in our legislative package a strong mandate to ensure universal service in the future—and I want to explain why.

We have become an information-rich society. Almost 100 percent of households have radio and television, and about 94 percent have telephone service. Three-quarters of households contain a VCR, about 60 percent have cable, and roughly 30 percent of households have personal computers.

As the information infrastructure expands in breadth and depth, so too will our understanding of the services that are deemed essential. This is not a matter of guaranteeing the right to play video games. It is a matter of guaranteeing access to essential services.

We cannot tolerate—nor in the long run can this nation afford—a society in which some children become fully educated and others do not; in which some adults have access to training and lifetime education, and others do not.

Nor can we permit geographic location to determine whether the information highway passes by your door. I've often spoken about my vision of a schoolchild in my home town of Carthage, Tennessee being able to come home, turn on her computer and plug into the Library of Congress. Carthage is a small town. Its population is only about 2,000. So let me emphasize the point: We must work to ensure that no geographic region of the United States, rural or urban, is left without access to broadband, interactive service. Yes, we support opening the local telephone exchange to competition. But we will not permit the dismantling of our present national networks.

All this won't be easy. It is critically important, therefore, that all carriers must be obliged to contribute, on an equitable and competitively neutral basis, to the preservation and advancement of universal service.

The responsibility to design specific measures to achieve these aims will be delegated to the Federal Communications Commission. But they will be required to do so. Our basic goal is simple: There *will* be universal service; that definition *will* evolve as technology and the infrastructure advance; and the FCC *will* get the job done.

Reforming our communications laws is only one element of the Administration's NII agenda. We'll be working hard to invest in critical NII technologies. We'll promote applications of the NII in areas such as scientific research, energy efficiency and advanced manufacturing. We'll work to deliver government services more efficiently. We'll also update our policies to make sure that privacy and copyright are protected in the networked world.

We'll help law enforcement agencies thwart criminals and terrorists who might use advanced telecommunications to commit crimes.

The Administration is working with industry to develop the new technologies needed for the National Information Infrastructure Initiative.

I have been working with the First Lady's Health Care Task Force, former Surgeon General C. Everett Koop, and others to develop ways we can use networks to improve the quality of health care.

Beginning this month, we are concentrating first on the legislative package I outlined earlier. We haven't invented all of the ideas it contains ourselves. Representatives Dingell and Brooks, Markey and Fields—and Senators Hollings, Inouye, and Danforth have all focused on these issues.

In many ways our legislative goals reflect or complement that work. We expect to introduce our legislative package shortly, and to work with Congress to ensure speedy passage this year of a bill that will stand the test of time.

Our efforts are not, of course, confined only to government. The people in this room, and the private sector in general, symbolize private enterprise.

Our economic future will depend, in a real sense, on your ability to grasp opportunity and turn it into concrete achievement.

As we move into the new era, we must never lose sight of our heritage of innovation and entrepreneurship.

In some ways, we appreciate that heritage more when we see countries without it. Last month, in Russia, I had the chance to see close up a country that tried to hold back the information age—a country that used to put armed guards in front of copiers. In a way we should be grateful it did; that helped strengthen the desire of the Russian people to end Communism.

My hope is that now Central and Eastern Europe can use technology and the free market to build democracy—not thwart it.

And my hope is that America, born in revolution, can lead the way in this new, peaceful world revolution.

Let's work on it together.

A few months ago, Toni Morrison won the Nobel Prize for Literature. It was a proud—and signal—moment for this country: recognition of an African-American woman who has communicated her insight and narrative power to readers all over the world.

In her acceptance speech, Toni Morrison used one version of an old story—a parable, really—to make an interesting point. It's of a blind, old woman renowned for her wisdom, and a boy who decides to play a trick on her. He captures a bird, brings it to her cupped in his hands, and says, "Old woman, is this bird alive or dead?"

If she says "Dead," he can set it free. If she says "Alive," the boy will crush the bird.

She thinks, and says, "The answer is in your hands."

Toni Morrison's point is that the future of *language* is in our hands.

As we enter this new millennium, we are learning a new language. It will be the *lingua franca* of the new age. It is made up of ones and zeros and bits and bytes. But as we master it . . . as we bring the digital revolution into our homes and schools . . . we will be able to communicate ideas, and information—in fact, entire Toni Morrison novels—with an ease never before thought possible.

We meet today on common ground, not to predict the future but to make firm the arrangements for its arrival. Let us master and develop this new language together.

The future really is in our hands.

Thank you.

Guidelines for Reform in Telecommunications Regulation

Michael Boskin

PRESIDENT BUSH'S COUNCIL OF ECONOMIC ADVISERS*

Today, technological innovations are making competition feasible in areas where it was previously considered infeasible. For example, one company has announced that it will soon have the technology to deliver movies over existing telephone wires. Similarly, cable television companies have the capability to provide customers with telephone service on their lines. The full benefits of these opportunities will be lost if the government maintains a regulatory structure that restricts competition and preserves artificial industry boundaries.

THE CURRENT STRUCTURE OF TELECOMMUNICATIONS REGULATION

The U.S. telecommunications industry is governed by Federal, State, and local regulatory agencies, with the Federal courts playing a special role. The FCC, the principal Federal regulatory agency governing telecommunications, is responsible for regulating interstate and international long-distance telephone services, managing non-Federal U.S. radio spectrum use, enforcing the rules applicable to the broadcasting industry, and establishing standards.

*This is an excerpt from the *Economic Report of the President* (Washington, DC: Government Printing Office, 1993).

A complicating factor in the Federal regulatory structure is the 1982 court settlement of the Federal Government's antitrust case against AT&T. This settlement, or consent decree, governed the subsequent breakup of AT&T. Under the decree, AT&T was required to divest itself of its 22 local telephone companies, which were then formed into 7 independent companies known as Regional Bell Operating Companies (RBOCs), or "Baby Bells." Most importantly, the decree also placed limits on the products and services the RBOCs could produce. Although some of these restrictions have been lifted, applications for interpretations of and waivers from the remaining restrictions have made the Federal courts a virtual second Federal regulator.

State regulatory commissions are responsible for regulating intrastate telephone services, but they also share their authority with Federal regulators because the same equipment is often used to provide both interstate and intrastate service. For example, the same telephone company switch that handles calls from San Francisco to Los Angeles may handle calls from San Francisco to Phoenix as well. But the first call is regulated by the State government and the second by the FCC. A system of rules and joint boards has been developed to help separate the Federal and State roles. The role of local government, on the other hand, has generally focused on franchising cable television service. The local government's role in cable television rate regulation will be expanded by new legislation, an issue discussed in detail below.

THE TRANSITION TO COMPETITION

One primary justification for limiting competition in the telecommunications industry has been the belief that certain markets are served by "natural monopolies," or single suppliers that can meet consumer needs more efficiently than multiple suppliers, often with appropriate regulation of prices and the number of competitors. A classic example is the costly duplication of facilities that would result from having competing electric utilities within the same geographic area. Based on the natural monopoly rationale, cable television services and local telephone services are provided by a single company in most communities.

But monopoly franchising and rate regulation can also have drawbacks. Protecting a monopoly may prevent potential competitors from implementing technologies that do not share the cost characteristics of a natural monopoly. For many years, regulators considered long-distance telephone service a natural monopoly, but the development of microwave technology allowed the provision of long-distance telephone service on a much smaller scale than had been previously possible. Almost 500 firms now provide long-distance services, ranging from those that serve a variety of customers on a national scale to those that target specialized business markets or operate on a much more limited geographic basis. New transmission technologies may achieve similar results in other markets that have been characterized as natural monopolies, such as cable television and local telephone service. In fact, government regulation, and not economic factors, may be the real bar to competition in those markets.

Competition drives firms to innovate and provide new services. In many telecommunications markets, competition is superior to continuing rate regulation and monopoly franchises, because competition can lower prices and increase the diversity of available services.

PROTECTING CONSUMERS IN THE TRANSITION

Markets in which competition has been precluded by government regulation cannot become competitive overnight. For example, providing local telephone service requires significant capital expenditures for new companies. Immediate deregulation of rates would allow a monopolist to increase rates without fear of an immediate response from a competitor. As a result, where changing technology and removal of governmental regulation make it possible for a regulated monopoly market to evolve into a competitive market, consumers must be protected from temporary price increases during the transition to competition. As part of the transition, incentive regulation is being used to encourage regulated companies to operate more efficiently.

In many areas, regulation has been used to enforce a system of cross-subsidies that keep prices low for certain classes of users, such as residential and rural telephone subscribers (Box 6). During a transition period—or longer if the subsidies are justified—these cross-subsidies should be replaced by direct subsidies.

When deregulatory policies create partially deregulated firms or allow regulated firms to enter unregulated markets, additional safeguards may be necessary to protect consumers and competition. For example, telephone companies in States that use cost-of-service regulation to determine rates may inappropriately transfer costs, or "cross-subsidize," from the unregulated to the regulated sector, artificially inflating prices for telephone service, and under some circumstances, reducing competition in the unregulated markets. In such cases, safeguards are necessary to ensure that customers are not subsidizing company activities in unregulated markets. Safeguards are also necessary to ensure that telephone companies do not design or misuse the network in ways that discriminate against companies selling related but unregulated services.

BOX 6.   IF DEREGULATION IS SO GREAT, WHY HAS MY PHONE BILL GONE UP?

When a telephone call is made across the country, a local phone company starts the call, a different local company completes the call, and a long-distance company carries the call between the two areas. Thus, the local phone network plays two roles: It provides phone service in a local area and access to long-distance service. Before 1984, AT&T, with its virtual monopoly over long-distance and local telephone service, carried nearly all phone calls. To determine the price of a long-distance call, Federal and State regulators had to allocate some of the costs of the local network to long-distance usage. With a higher share of the costs attributed to long-distance calling, long-distance prices would be higher and local service prices lower.

Political pressures resulted in a shift of costs to the long-distance operations of the telephone network, so that local rates were kept artificially low. This regulatory shift of costs resulted in prices that led to an inefficient use of the network. The cost of providing a customer access to a long-distance company is a *fixed cost,* unrelated to the number of long-distance minutes that are used. However, these fixed costs were reflected in the per-minute charge for service, a price that should only reflect the extra, or *marginal cost,* of providing the service. The higher long-distance rates resulting from this policy caused users to reduce long-distance calling and prompted the entry of other companies.

Realizing the problems arising from this pricing policy, the FCC began reform in the late 1970s. Instead of including the costs of access in long-distance prices, some access costs are now recovered through a fixed monthly *subscriber line charge* added to the local telephone bill. The FCC has been gradually shifting access costs for residential customers to the subscriber line charge since 1983. The monthly price for local telephone service increased 3.1 percent annually between 1983 and 1989 in real terms. For some, this increase has meant higher phone bills. But interstate long-distance prices *declined* 9.8 percent annually in the same period as a result of increased competition, the repricing of access, and technological improvements.

REFORMING TELECOMMUNICATIONS REGULATION

The transition from regulation to competition in telecommunications began over 20 years ago. Technological change, actions taken by the FCC, and the breakup of AT&T in 1984 have allowed many new firms to enter the telecommunications industry. For example, in 1970 AT&T's manufacturing subsidiary, Western Electric, provided almost all of the company's equipment needs and the equipment used by its customers. FCC and court decisions to allow customers to use non-AT&T equipment and the separation of the RBOCs from the manufacturing subsidiary, coupled with rapid advances in electronics, created a competitive market for equipment. For instance, AT&T's U.S. market share of sales for private branch exchanges (telephone exchange equipment for use within businesses) fell from 80 percent in 1970 to 28 percent in 1989.

Many current regulations may continue to inhibit competition in the telecommunications industry, however. Even with safeguards in place, the RBOCs are limited in their ability to enter unregulated markets. Moreover, as discussed below, the cumbersome process by which the government manages the electromagnetic spectrum continues to slow the development of new technologies that could lead to greater competition in local telephone markets. Competition in local telephone markets could make regulatory safeguards unnecessary. Competition would make it unprofitable for telephone companies to discriminate against customers wanting to connect with a local network, because dissatisfied customers could simply switch to alternative networks. Similarly, competition would undermine attempts by one firm to use one business to cross-subsidize another.

The government decides not only which services the local telephone companies can provide but also which services cable operators and broadcasters can provide. For example, three television broadcast networks—CBS, NBC, and ABC—have not been allowed to participate fully in the development, ownership, and syndication of programming for broadcast and cable television since 1970. At that time, the networks' over 90 percent share of the prime-time viewing audience created concern that the networks had excessive bargaining power over program producers, especially small independent producers. These financial interest and syndication rules are unnecessarily restrictive, given that the share of prime-time viewing the major networks command has fallen to 62 percent and that there are now a multiplicity of alternative broadcast outlets for program producers. Furthermore, an increasing fraction of program production is being done by a small number of large firms. Therefore, the rules should be eased to allow greater participation by networks to promote competition, while assuring that legitimately small independent producers are not subject to anticompetitive conduct. The FCC modified the rules slightly in 1991. A Federal Appeals Court, however, has questioned the manner in which the modified rules were devised and has sent the matter back to the FCC. The future of the rules remains uncertain.

While the goal of regulation has been to protect consumers, barring businesses from entering new markets may be reducing the incentive of firms to invest in new telecommunications technologies. Furthermore, policymaking in telecommunications is stymied because businesses protected from competition can use the political process to prevent entry by new competitors, while at the same time demanding freedom to enter other markets. To break this deadlock, protect consumers, and promote competition, reform of the current telecommunications regulatory policy is necessary.

MANAGING THE ELECTROMAGNETIC SPECTRUM

The electromagnetic spectrum is the foundation of many telecommunications services. Radio and television broadcasters, cellular telephone services, police and fire communications, air traffic control, and taxi dispatchers all rely on the spectrum. Because the range of frequencies within which these services can be provided is limited, spectrum is a very valuable resource. The FCC, which is responsible for managing the portion of the spectrum not used by the Federal Government, determines which services will be allowed to use a given spectrum band (known as "allocating" the spectrum), and who will be assigned licenses for their use.

While the FCC has a legitimate role in defining the terms under which spectrum is used in order to prevent users from interfering with each other, it is not well-suited to judge whether, for example, paging systems have a higher social value than taxi dispatching. The current administrative process for determining how bands are used is slow and inflexible, constraining the introduction of new technologies and the development of competitive markets. Cellular telephone technology illustrates this problem. The spectrum allocation process began in 1968, yet the first commercial cellular license was not assigned until 1982. Also, the number of licenses is fixed, limiting competition to two cellular franchises in each local market.

Currently, the FCC typically assigns licenses to use a given service either after comparative hearings or by lottery. Comparative hearings are time-consuming, trial-like procedures. Companies that place value on a license will naturally want the FCC to assign it to them. The result is large expenditures by applicants to acquire the license and a long delay before the license is assigned. The lottery system is also cumbersome, involving large numbers of applicants attempting to "win" a license. When an assignment is made, the chosen licensee often does not provide the service. Instead, licenses are frequently sold after the initial assignment. *Since licenses are often sold to other users, the FCC could hold an auction for licenses, eliminating the current cumbersome process and generating revenue for the U.S. Treasury.* The bidder attaching the greatest value to the spectrum license would receive it, and the step of holding lotteries or comparative hearings would be eliminated.

To permit more efficient use of the spectrum the FCC could allow the licenses it auctions not only to be resold, but also to be reassigned by the licenseholder for a different use. This approach would offer licensees the maximum flexibility in using the spectrum, subject only to prohibitions on interfering with other spectrum users. Flexibility in the use of the spectrum would also encourage users to develop technologies that conserve the amount of the spectrum used.

REMOVING ARTIFICIAL BARRIERS TO INNOVATION

Like the spectrum management system, the consent decree governing the breakup of AT&T limits innovation and competition in telecommunications markets. Among other things, the 1982 decree contained provisions that prevented the RBOCS from manufacturing telecommunications equipment, providing information services, and providing most long-distance services. The problems of cross-subsidization and discriminatory use of a monopoly network were two important reasons for initially limiting participation of the RBOCs in unregulated markets.

In 1991 a Federal court struck down the provision in the decree that barred the RBOCs from providing information services, allowing these companies to begin offering services such as message and database services. Previously forced to act as conduits for other providers of information services, the RBOCs can now provide these services themselves. Because these companies have developed expertise in communications networks and can take advantage of the efficiencies, or "economies of scope," that make it cheaper to provide multiple services over a single network than to have many specialized networks, they will increase competition for information services.

The benefits of having competing services will be reduced, however, if the RBOCs limit competition by engaging in cross-subsidization or by denying other firms access to the local telephone network. These problems must be continuously monitored by Federal and State regulatory agencies. To reduce the concern about cross-subsidization and discrimination, the FCC has adopted rules governing cost allocation and rules that attempt to assure open access to various components of the local telephone network on a timely and nondiscriminatory basis. If problems arise, these rules may have to be strengthened even further. The rules will continue to be necessary until competition is fully developed in local telephone markets.

The RBOCs are still barred from manufacturing telephone equipment, a category the courts have interpreted as including related research and development. The ban effectively prevents seven of the largest U.S. telecommunications companies from developing innovative technologies and otherwise competing in this market. Supporters of the ban fear that the RBOCs will attempt either to transfer manufacturing costs to the regulated sector or to engage in "self-dealing" by selling equipment to their affiliated telephone companies at inflated prices, raising the costs of regulated telephone service and reducing competition in equipment manufacturing.

The FCC and many States have begun using incentive regulation that should help to alleviate these problems by making it more difficult for the RBOCs to pass added costs on to telephone ratepayers. Also, a competitive market for telecommunications equipment should provide competitors and regulators with adequate information on the market value of equipment, to allow them to monitor the self-dealing problem.

While the consent decree prevents the RBOCs from participating in certain businesses, the Cable Communications Policy Act of 1984 and related FCC regulations prevent local telephone companies from operating cable television systems (except in certain rural communities). This ban remains in place, even though virtually all communities with cable television have only one franchised operator, and average rates for the most popular basic cable service have increased 36.5 percent, in real terms, since 1986 when the act effectively barred regulation in most communities. Although this increase may be due in part to the growing number of channels available, it may also reflect the presence of market power.

The solution pursued in the Cable Television Consumer Protection and Competition Act of 1992 is to allow local governments to regulate prices for basic cable television service in almost all communities. Regulating prices, however, does not solve the underlying problem, which is a lack of competition. This approach also overestimates the ability of regulatory authorities to establish rates that approximate competitive prices. The danger is that in the attempt to regulate prices they will simultaneously diminish the variety and quality of cable programming.

The preferred alternative is to promote competition that lowers prices and provides alternative sources of television programming. Having already invested in some of the fixed plant necessary to provide video services, telephone companies are the most likely competitors for incumbent cable operators. The FCC's "video dial-tone" policy, adopted in July 1992, allows local telephone companies to act as conduits for carrying television and other video services by other companies. *Legislation is needed, however, to remove the provisions in the 1984 Cable Act that prevent telephone companies from actually becoming full participants in providing programming.* Such legislation may create an incentive for telephone companies to construct the infrastructure necessary for combining telephone and video services. Whether there is a demand for the services that such an infrastructure can provide will not be known until the barriers to competition are removed.

COMPETITION IN LOCAL TELEPHONE SERVICES

State regulators have begun to approve competition from alternative local service providers that typically provide private fiber optic links between long-distance telephone companies and large businesses. In 1989, the New York Public Service Commission ordered New York Telephone to interconnect with alternative local service providers. The FCC recently modified its rules to allow these providers to interconnect their private lines with the interstate facilities of local telephone companies. The policy of expanded interconnection increases the possibility of competition for large customers. It recognizes that residential customers may be served by a regulated monopoly for the near future, but is laying the groundwork for competition even in residential markets.

Technological changes suggest that competition can develop in the local telecommunications market. Many businesses have already switched to private networks for intracompany calls. Expanding wireless technologies, such as that for cellular telephone service, do not necessarily have the characteristics of a natural monopoly and represent potential competition for local telephone companies. Competition for local telephone service would be further enhanced if cable television companies were permitted to provide telephone service.

An important factor affecting competition in the future is the policy of "universal service"—access for all residential users to a basic level of telephone service at affordable rates. This policy has been motivated by both equity concerns and the understanding that each telephone user benefits from being connected to as many people as possible. To make telephone service universal, basic services are often priced lower than the cost of providing the service. Other services, such as touchtone or call waiting, are priced somewhat higher than costs to compensate for losses on the underpriced basic services. Residential customers are usually the recipients of these "subsidized" services.

One problem with this system of cross-subsidies is that companies—even those less efficient than the regulated incumbent—may be able to undercut the regulated price and still earn a profit. If the regulated monopolist cannot adjust its prices in response to this competition, the inefficient companies will remain in business. This pricing policy could ultimately cause many of the monopoly's customers to switch to the new entrants, meaning that rates for some of the subsidized services would have to be increased.

If regulated carriers are not permitted to respond to competition, they may find that their rates do not cover the costs of providing service to their remaining customers—most likely small businesses and residential customers. Restricting competition is not the answer to the problem, however.

The best way to avoid the perverse results cross-subsidies can create is to give the regulated companies greater freedom to respond to competitive entry. Doing so will discourage entry by inefficient competitors and only efficient competitors will survive. Any perceived need for subsidies can be achieved directly—for example, by charging all interconnecting companies a fee that supports universal service and targeting the subsidy to the groups that need it.

COMPETITION IN LONG-DISTANCE SERVICES

In a series of decisions that began in the 1970s, the FCC and the courts have opened the long-distance markets to competition. Chart 5 shows that since its breakup in 1984, AT&T's market share of long-distance calling minutes has fallen from 84 percent to 60 percent. The FCC estimates that some 480 firms currently provide interstate long-distance services, while over 90 percent of all telephone customers now have equal access to multiple long-distance providers. Customers have shown a willingness to respond to competitive service offerings: Approximately 15 percent of all residential customers switched to a new long-distance carrier in 1991.

CHART 5   AT&T's Market Share

AT&T's market share has declined significantly since the breakup in 1984.

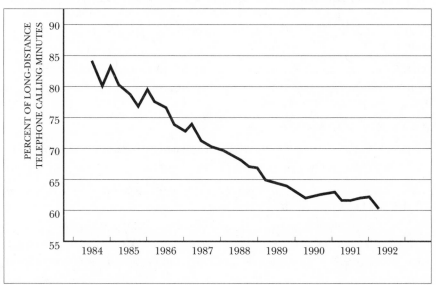

Source: Federal Communications Commission.

Except for AT&T, the FCC does not regulate the rates of interstate long-distance companies. To promote the efficiency of rate regulation while still protecting consumers, the FCC introduced price cap regulation for AT&T in 1989 and for the interstate services of local telephone companies in 1991. Several States have also introduced incentive regulation for intrastate services. In 1991, increasing competition led the FCC to eliminate price cap regulation for AT&T's large business services.

Price cap regulation is still in place for AT&T's residential, small business, and 800 number services. For these services AT&T must give the FCC at least 45 days notice before it can offer new services or prices. The ability of most long-distance customers to easily switch among long-distance companies that provide similar geographic coverage and service quality suggests that the FCC should consider relaxing the constraints of price cap regulation on AT&T. However, some form of regulation would still be appropriate for communities that do not have a competitive long-distance market.

SUMMARY

□ Government policies that protect consumers while allowing firms to compete in new lines of business will promote an advanced telecommunications infrastructure.

□ The current system for allocating the electromagnetic spectrum hampers the development and implementation of new technologies that could create competition for existing monopoly service providers such as cable television and local telephone service.

□ Because competition in long-distance telephone service is increasing, some of the remaining regulations governing AT&T could be relaxed.

QUESTIONS FOR ANALYSIS

1. Why has the telephone industry been regulated by the federal and state governments? What are the benefits of such regulation?

2. What are the drawbacks of regulation of the telephone industry? What would be the benefits of deregulation?

3. According to Vice President Gore, the investment required to build the information superhighway should be made by the private sector of the economy. Why shouldn't the government supply the funds? Don't the benefits extend to the entire nation?

4. Mr. Gore proposes that the responsibility for designing specific measures to carry out government's aims be delegated to the Federal Communications Commission. Why should the Federal Communications Commission, or any other federal agency, be involved? Why not let free enterprise alone in this area?

5. According to the Vice President, "We must work to ensure that no geographic region of the United States, rural or urban, is left without access to broadband, interactive service." Why? Doesn't this depend on the costs involved?

6. Is the information superhighway a natural monopoly? Why or why not? In formulating public policy, what difference does it make whether the information superhighway is a natural monopoly?

7. Chart 5 shows that AT&T's market share has decreased from about 85 percent in 1984 to about 60 percent in 1992. Why did this occur? Does this trend imply that it will not be long before the market for long-distance telephone service is perfectly competitive? Why or why not?

8. According to President Bush's Council of Economic Advisers, "Competition drives firms to innovate and provide new services. In many telecommunications markets, competition is superior to continuing rate regulation and monopoly franchises. . . . " Why did President Bush's Council of Economic Advisers believe this to be true? Do you agree? Why or why not?

9. President Bush's Council of Economic Advisers favored an auction for licenses, rather than comparative hearings or a lottery, as a means of allocating the electromagnetic spectrum. What are the advantages of an auction, according to President Bush's Council of Economic Advisers? Do you agree that auctions are best for this purpose? Why or why not?

10. The number of firms in the defense industry has declined in recent years. Why has the number of firms in the telephone industry increased while the number of firms in the defense industry decreased? Is this because of shifts in demand? Is it due to technological change? If an increase in the number of telephone firms is healthy for the economy, can a decrease in the number of defense firms be healthy as well? Why or why not?

PART FOUR

ANTITRUST

POLICY

For over a century, the United States has had antitrust laws on the books. In recent years, many have asserted that vigorous antitrust enforcement hurts innovation, which is so important to our economy. In the first article, Anne Bingaman, head of the Antitrust Division of the U.S. Department of Justice, argues that this is not true. In the second article, the Antitrust Division describes eight recent cases. In the third article, the *New York Times* comments on Judge Stanley Sporkin's rejection of a consent decree involving Microsoft Corporation, the huge software producer.

Innovation and Antitrust

ANNE K. BINGAMAN*

It is a great pleasure to appear before the Commonwealth Club. You have long been recognized as the foremost public affairs speakers' forum in our nation, and I am enormously honored to be here. Today, I would like to address a topic particularly relevant in the Bay area—home to two of the greatest research universities in the world, the University of California at Berkeley and Stanford, and to hundreds, if not thousands, of high-tech companies. The world is envious and California makes this nation proud of the genius, drive, and products of those companies.

My subject is one often casually discussed and remarked upon, but, to my mind, not well enough understood—the relationship between the technological innovation so central to our economy, on the one hand, and vigorous, but sound, antitrust enforcement, on the other.

From time to time, it is asserted that vigorous antitrust enforcement hurts innovation by preventing the concentration of assets that spurs innovation. Competitive research is derided as duplicative and wasteful. Recently, the argument has been given an international flavor—it is asserted that the firms of other nations succeed because they are allowed to engage in cartel activity and collaborative research denied to U.S. firms because of the antitrust laws. As a general proposition, I believe that those views are wrong

*This is a speech given before the Commonwealth Club of California on July 29, 1994. Anne K. Bingaman is Assistant Attorney General.

and that innovation is *not* advanced by a policy of permitting cartel activity. Indeed, my core belief is that the U.S. economy today is the most dynamic, creates the most jobs, and produces the highest level of innovation precisely *because* we as a nation committed long ago to a policy of vigorous but sound antitrust enforcement. My thesis before you today, then, is that antitrust enforcement is as essential to innovation and economic growth in the twenty-first century as it has been in the twentieth—and that vigorous but reasonable antitrust enforcement is a crucial component of the fight to keep America competitive in international and high-tech markets.

Before I explain these views, however, it is imperative that you have a clear understanding of how modern antitrust law is applied. I need not go back to the legislative histories of the Sherman and Clayton Acts to ascertain whether those laws originally reflected an animus against large corporations. If they did, that is simply no longer the case. Congress drafted the antitrust laws in sufficiently general terms to delegate to the courts the task of developing an antitrust jurisprudence that is consistent with contemporary concepts of economic efficiency and consumer welfare. And the courts and federal antitrust enforcement agencies have accepted that responsibility.

As a result, current antitrust law recognizes the economic concepts of economies of scale and scope. Thus, on particular facts, a merger that eliminates competition between significant rivals may nevertheless pass antitrust muster if the parties truly can demonstrate that the merger is necessary to achieve substantial efficiency that will enhance consumer welfare. In the same vein, it is now clearly true that antitrust typically does not treat as inherently suspect horizontal or vertical joint ventures designed to integrate substantial business assets. This is especially true with respect to those types of joint ventures that are most directly involved in innovation. Despite the fact that such joint ventures had rarely been challenged under the antitrust laws, in 1984 Congress took action to lessen what was perceived to be an inhibitory effect of antitrust enforcement by making it clear that research and development joint ventures were to be judged under a rule of reason test. Last year, Congress took similar action with respect to production joint ventures. Whatever may have been the case previously, the time has long since passed when legitimate joint or collaborative activity among rivals could be viewed as inherently suspect under our antitrust laws.

With this understanding of contemporary antitrust policy firmly in mind, let me return to the original issue posed: is enforcement of modern antitrust policies that recognize economies of scale and scope, as well as the risk reduction benefits of collaborative action, inconsistent with the promotion of innovation? Lest you be left in doubt, for me the answer squarely is "no."

The economist Joseph Schumpeter was one of the first to articulate a theory that firms with stable and substantial market power were the most likely to invest in innovation. In particular, he suggested that firms with substantial market power—those that did not have to think in terms of short-range response to rivals—were the most likely to invest in long-range research and development. While not implausible as a matter of theory, Schumpeter's thesis has been severely undercut by real world developments, as Professor F. M. Scherer's 1984 book, *Innovation and Growth,* demonstrated. There, Professor Scherer showed that the largest corporations accomplish less in producing innovation than smaller enterprises, as measured by R & D expenditures, once some threshhold points are passed.

Further, in a world driven by rapid changes in technology, other empirical evidence available to us now indicates that the firms that prosper are more likely to be those that face fierce rivalry in their home markets than the sheltered monopolists. In a very real sense, it seems, the fear of being left behind is more likely to spur innovation than the security bred of stable market power.

This subject is extensively dealt with in Professor Michael Porter's recently acclaimed work, *The Competitive Advantage of Nations.* Noting that the need for antitrust enforcement has been questioned because of the globalization of industries and the view that domestic firms must merge or closely collaborate to gain economies of scale, Professor Porter found such claims to be inconsistent with available empirical evidence in the ten nations that he and his colleagues at the Harvard Business School studied. Rejecting arguments for lenient merger and cartel policies, he states that

"in fact, creating a dominant domestic competitor rarely results in international competitive advantage. Firms that do not have to compete at home rarely succeed abroad. Economies of scale are best gained by selling globally, not through dominating the home market. . . ." *Id.* at 662.

Observing that corporate managers often support lenient merger and collaboration policies because it is a "tempting way to raise short-term profits," Professor Porter views such policies as the path to national decline. Pointing to evidence that "active domestic rivalry is strongly associated with international success," he concludes that "a strong antitrust policy, especially in the area of horizontal mergers, alliances and collusive behavior, is essential to the role of upgrading any economy." *Id.* at 663.

Those of us who have spent our lives in antitrust were not surprised by Professor Porter's findings. The fundamental thesis of strong antitrust enforcement is that rivalry, not market power, fosters innovation and efficiency over the long run. For that reason, among others, this nation has committed its public policy for over a century to the view that antitrust enforcement promotes, rather than impedes, innovation. Innovation itself, of course, can and does take many forms. The term is applied to basic scientific breakthroughs, important commercial inventions, product modifications and new production techniques. All are important to society. Innovation, whether in the form of improved product quality and variety, or production efficiency that allows lower prices, is a powerful engine for enhanced consumer welfare. By prohibiting private restraints that impede entry or mute rivalry, antitrust seeks to create an economic environment in which the entrepreneurial initiative that is the hallmark of the U.S. economy can flourish, and opportunities for bringing innovations to market can continue to be exploited by the multitude of private actors in this freest of free market economies.

Acknowledging that an occasional natural monopoly may arise, and that enormous economies of scale may inevitably lead to few rivals in some markets, we remain skeptical about any general policy of eschewing rivalry in favor of collaborative research and development. This nation's experience teaches that innovation comes from unpredictable sources—from individuals and small firms as well as giant conglomerates. And this diversity in the sources of innovation is not limited to the nineteenth and early twentieth centuries, when change arguably occurred less rapidly.

If you compare the major firms in the computer and telecommunications industries in the 1950s, '60s, and '70s with the major firms today, you will see that rapid technological change can create opportunities for new entrants and individual achievement. It is not difficult to make a list of large U.S. firms who once possessed some degree of market power, only to fall back when confronted by more innovative rivals. It includes IBM, GM, big steel, major airlines, Citicorp, and you would undoubtedly think of additional examples. Happily, a number of those firms have demonstrated the ability to rebound, but their improved performance unquestionably was stimulated by the rivalry they have encountered.

The task of antitrust is not to prejudge winners but to make sure that private restraints do not narrow the potential sources of innovation. By preserving an economic climate that allows efficient sources of innovation to prosper, be they small or large, antitrust promotes the economic and sociopolitical values that have been the backbone of the success of the American economy.

An effective antitrust enforcement program promotes innovation by, among other things, reducing barriers to entry. When antitrust enforcement is a reality, potential entrants have less reason to fear market exclusion by existing firms. Antitrust enforcement can also act to prevent horizontal or vertical mergers that create non-efficiency based advantages for incumbent market leaders. For these and other reasons, potential entrants are more likely to invest the capital and effort needed for innovation when they have a "fair" chance at success, that is, when they have a chance to compete on the economic merits of their products or services.

We have brought two major cases in recent months to guarantee exactly this result. The first was against Pilkington, a British company that has maintained a monopoly throughout the world over the past three decades in float glass technology, the lowest cost method of manufacturing float glass used for automobiles and buildings.

While Pilkington may well have achieved its monopoly position fair and square—through patented innovations—it later cemented and abused its float glass technology monopoly through unfair and unlawful means. Among other things, Pilkington entered into patent and know-how license agreements with its principal rivals, which discouraged the very firms most likely to develop and use their own innovations in float glass technology. Pilkington continued to enforce against those would-be competitors very restrictive license provisions to thwart competition long after its patents had expired. As a result, Pilkington's major competitors—including such leading U.S. float glass manufacturers as PPG, Guardian and Ford—were largely foreclosed from the important international float glass technology market, and consumers were deprived of the benefits of more efficient production techniques and higher quality glass.

In May, the Department reached a settlement and proposed consent decree now before the U.S. District Court for the District of Arizona, that will end Pilkington's unlawful practices and thus free up the market in world float glass technology. We estimate that the settlement will not only stimulate innovation in this industry, but will generate anywhere from $150 million to $1.25 billion in exports through the year 2000 of American goods and services used to build new float glass plants coming on stream throughout the world. The *Pilkington* case is a paradigm for how U.S. antitrust enforcement can foster innovation and open export markets previously closed by anticompetitive practices.

On July 15, the Department filed a Complaint against, and a proposed settlement with, Microsoft for engaging in practices that we believed stifled innovation in another technology market: the market for operating systems used in personal computers.

Based on an extensive investigation, the Complaint alleges that Microsoft had gained a dominant position in its market by marketing operating systems that the public clearly wanted; but, as in *Pilkington,* Microsoft then chose to employ various unlawful practices to cement its dominance and thwart innovation.

In particular, the *Microsoft* Complaint challenges a combination of provi-

sions used by Microsoft in its license agreements with PC manufacturers—
"per processor" royalties that taxed competing operating systems, lengthy
terms, and huge minimum commitments, strictly enforced—that had the
effect of locking competing operating systems out of the market. While impeding competitors' access to the PC manufacturing channel, the Complaint further alleges that Microsoft also tried to get developers of
applications programs to sign non-disclosure agreements that would have
had the effect of preventing them from writing programs for those competing operating systems.

Our proposed consent decree, now before the United States District
Court in the District of Columbia, will end each and every one of these
challenged practices. It will also prevent Microsoft from engaging in other
practices, such as charging licensees on a lump sum basis or tying the sales
of its operating systems to other products—all practices that could produce
anticompetitive effects similar to the unlawful practices in which Microsoft
had previously engaged.

In short, the proposed *Microsoft* consent decree does precisely what the
antitrust laws are designed to do: provide a level playing field so that all
competitors have a fair shot at success on the merits.

Antitrust actions in previous Administrations have been central in promoting innovation and growth in the U.S. economy. The best, and most
important example in U.S. history is the challenge and eventual breakup of
AT&T—still an ongoing saga in Congress and before the United States District Court for the District of Columbia.

Prior to the Antitrust Division's challenge in that lawsuit, most of the nation was served by an integrated monopolist that faced little or no rivalry in
the various telecommunications markets in which it operated. The quality
of service provided by that integrated monopolist was not terrible; indeed,
it was considered to be good, at least when compared to that provided in
other countries by their monopoly providers. However, consumer choice
was hardly the hallmark of the integrated AT&T system. For the most part,
improvements appeared at a pace dictated by AT&T and its lengthy depreciation schedules, not by the needs of business or residential customers,
and certainly not by competition.

The divestiture required in the Modified Final Judgment in *U.S. v.
AT&T* separated the local telephone companies from AT&T's long-distance service and equipment manufacturing firms. The newly independent
local phone companies were required to provide access to AT&T's long distance rivals that was functionally equivalent to that provided to AT&T.
Other equipment manufacturers now had an opportunity to sell their
wares on the basis of quality, cost and efficiency to the divested local operating companies, AT&T's emerging long distance rivals, and users of telecommunications services.

In terms of innovation, the results have been spectacular. Fiber optic cable was promoted by Corning to Sprint and MCI. Advantages over the older cable technology for certain purposes are sufficiently clear that it is now widely deployed in local as well as long distance phone companies. The advances in fiber optics triggered responsive unexpected improvement in coaxial cable, through digital compression and other techniques. At the same time, satellite and other wireless technologies have advanced to offer still more options. How will these technologies be deployed in the Information Superhighway of the future? In what proportions will they be used? Which will be dominant? Which will be complementary? Which will be rendered obsolete? Nobody can speak with certainty on such issues. But one thing is clear—intelligent antitrust enforcement action served as a catalyst to technological innovation in telecommunications that is extraordinary by any measure. And the best technology is most likely to succeed in a competitive environment.

Antitrust has an important role in preserving the rivalry that spurs innovation. In addition to lowering barriers to entry, it can be used to prohibit collaborative conduct that is designed to, or has the effect of, retarding innovation. *U.S. v. Automobile Manufacturers Assoc. Inc.* (C.D. Cal. 1969), was a classic case of that type. The case, which was settled by consent decree, alleged that the major U.S. automobile producers entered into an agreement that required all members to grant royalty-free patent licenses to each other and to only take patent licenses from outsiders if all members could obtain the same license under the same terms. The effect of this agreement was to eliminate rivalry in pollution-abatement innovation. Since no one had to fear being left behind, the spur to innovate was blunted.

The Antitrust Division will continue to be alert to agreements designed to, or that have the effect of, retarding rivalry with respect to innovation, and will not hesitate to challenge them. At the same time, however, we offer a business review procedure that allows parties to obtain a statement of our enforcement intentions with respect to prospective conduct. Indeed, we recently issued a business review letter indicating that we would not challenge a joint venture designed to facilitate research on fuel cell development as an alternate energy source.

The arguments of those who endorse collaborative research and the development of national champions as the generally preferred method of advancement find little support in recent developments. Where commercial success depends on such ephemeral factors as consumer taste for services or products that do not yet exist and the pace and direction of new technology, there appears to be a definite advantage to fostering a competitive approach rather than developing a national champion. The history of HDTV technology development provides a vivid example. You may recall that both Japan and the European Community promoted a single chosen technological approach well in advance of technological readiness or clear expression of consumer desires.

By contrast, the U.S. approach was to promote rivalry in technological design. Initially, the chosen instrument approach to technology seemed to pay off, as both Japan and the EC developed prototypes before we did. However, there is often a difference between getting the quickest start and winning the race, a fact sadly recognized by Boston Red Sox fans over the years, and that is what appears to have happened with respect to HDTV development. At this point, neither the Japanese nor European systems have experienced any significant commercial success in their home markets. More importantly, there appears to be a growing consensus that a digital approach such as that developed by the various U.S. rivals will be superior to the analog systems utilized by the Japanese and Europeans.

I discuss the post-AT&T divestiture developments and the HDTV history as cautionary tales, not as proof that a chosen instrument approach to innovation can never succeed. I am not so presumptuous as to make such a categorical claim. These tales, however, and others that I will relate in a moment, reinforce my view that competitive markets are likely to be superior to government planning in bringing about innovation that will satisfy consumer tastes and needs.

The salutary effect of competition on innovation has been demonstrated repeatedly in this country when a variety of previously regulated industries have been deregulated, either in whole or in part. I have already talked about telecommunications in connection with the AT&T divestiture. But I would be remiss if I failed to credit at least part of the dynamism of that industry to the deregulatory actions of the FCC over the past twenty-five years. Deregulation of land and air transportation also has allowed consumers to reap the benefits of innovations in those fields. Freed of limitations on entry, trucking firms and airlines have deployed new and specialized types of equipment based on consumer desires and efficiency. In both of these fields, fierce service rivalry has produced substantial benefits to consumers. For example, the entry and subsequent growth of Southwest Airlines stimulated price competition that has benefited air travelers. Our securities industry provides another example of the benefits of competition. Since Congress reduced economic regulation of the securities industry, consumers of such services have saved hundreds of millions of dollars annually. Numerous strong firms compete for business on the basis of quality as well as price. Employing the latest developments in computer technology, they seek to provide consumers with added value.

In response to those who point to certain foreign successes as proof that a collaborative or chosen instrument approach to innovation is the better way, I make the following response. It is not foreign monopoly airlines that are seeking to exploit their superior efficiency by expanding international competition. Rather, it is our airlines, toughened by domestic rivalry, that are willing and anxious to compete on a global basis. Similarly, the U.S. telecommunications industry, both carriers and equipment manufacturers, is leading the way in attempts to modernize telecommunications capabilities around the world. And, while it is by no means a one-way street, U.S. banks and securities firms seem to be more willing and anxious to compete abroad than their foreign counterparts who have developed in a more sheltered environment. There are many other examples of industries in which the rough and tumble of U.S. competition has prepared our firms to play a leading role in international commerce. U.S. law firms, accounting firms, consulting firms, and advertising firms have all been, in general, more willing than their foreign counterparts to expand abroad. They have proved to be at least as adept as their foreign counterparts in innovating to meet the new and changing requirements of international trade.

Do not be misled by the fact that many of these examples involve services. Rivalry in domestic product markets also benefits U.S. manufacturers in their international efforts. Can there be any doubt that the relatively open U.S. automobile markets placed great pressure on U.S. auto firms to improve their products and efficiency? As a result, with better products, produced in factories that adopted recent innovations, the U.S. firms seem poised to regain international preeminence, or at least a place in the very first rank of auto producers. Telecommunications equipment, aircraft, agricultural equipment, pharmaceuticals, computers (hardware and software), medical equipment, and entertainment are other examples of U.S. products and services that excel in international competition at least in part because of the fierce quality rivalry that characterizes our domestic markets. Indeed, your own Silicon Valley is home to a company which has made the United States the world leader in the use of computers for animation, Silicon Graphics. Other U.S. companies, such as Lucas Films and Industrial Light and Magic, produce the computer-generated special effects that are seen in films such as Jurassic Park and Terminator 2. And many other industries and companies could be cited which have given this country a position in world markets second to none.

As you can plainly see, I have at least two strongly held beliefs: innovation is critically important to the advancement of this nation's economic interests; and, in general, the competitive approach is superior to the collaborative approach in terms of producing commercially valuable innovation. I do not, however, want you to lose sight of some important qualifications to my general preference for competition in the effort to foster innovation. I have already noted them, but they bear repetition. I recognize that there may be situations in which collaboration in R&D or production may be necessary or simply more efficient than unilateral efforts. We are well aware of the benefits of risk reduction and economies of scale and scope that attend some joint ventures. In some rare instances, risk reduction or economies of scale may even justify a unified approach to research and development, but we will require those who promote that view to demonstrate why competition would be an inferior approach.

A similar reservation is appropriate with respect to government involvement in innovation. My celebration of the competitive benefits that usually flow to consumers from economic deregulation should not be viewed as denying *any* role to government. There is most definitely a role for government in the innovative process. The market does not do everything well. Appropriately, we do not rely solely on the market to protect us from unsafe products and workplaces, or from despoliation of the environment. In the same manner, government can provide an innovation vision, can suggest priorities, can provide an infrastructure through education and standardization, and in some cases can accelerate research in areas of potentially great value to society by providing planning and, in some instances, financial assistance. But, where consumer desires are uncertain, and the technology is as yet undeveloped, we should not lose sight of our experience—competition is generally the most effective means of promoting the innovation so critical to our nation's success in the international economic community of the twenty-first century. Sound, reasoned and vigorous antitrust enforcement can make its own significant contribution to that goal, and the Antitrust Division will remain a vital part of that effort.

Eight Recent
Antitrust Cases

ANTITRUST DIVISION, U.S. DEPARTMENT OF JUSTICE*

ONE: THERMAL FAX PAPER

After a two year investigation coordinated with Canadian antitrust officials, the Division and its Canadian counterpart in July 1994 brought criminal charges under their respective laws against an international cartel that had fixed prices in the $120 million a year thermal fax paper market. The Division's criminal information charged a Japanese corporation, two U.S. subsidiaries of Japanese firms and an executive of one of the firms with conspiring to charge higher prices to thermal fax paper customers in North America. Thermal fax paper is used primarily by small businesses and home fax machine owners. The defendants pleaded guilty and agreed to pay $6.4 million in fines.

The Division and Canadian officials are continuing the joint investigation into the fax paper industry under the U.S.-Canada Mutual Legal Assistance Treaty. This case was the Division's first criminal prosecution of a major Japanese corporation headquartered in Tokyo as well as the first to be coordinated with Canadian authorities, and illustrates the type of international antitrust cooperation that will occur more frequently in the future.

*This includes excerpts from the *Antitrust Division Annual Report for Fiscal Year 1994* (Washington, D.C.: Government Printing Office, 1995).

TWO: INDUSTRIAL DIAMONDS

In February 1994, the Division obtained an indictment of General Electric, DeBeers Centenary and two individuals charging them with conspiring to raise list prices in the $500 million a year industrial diamond industry. The two corporate defendants account for 80 percent of the industrial diamond market and allegedly fixed prices by secretly exchanging information about intended price hikes. The price increases went into effect worldwide in February and March of 1992. DeBeers and the two individuals remained overseas and beyond the reach of the U.S. courts. Trial of General Electric began in October 1994, but charges were dismissed after the presentation of the Government's case. The Division remains committed to aggressive criminal antitrust enforcement against international price-fixing cartels that raise prices to consumers and businesses in the United States.

THREE: GLASS MANUFACTURING TECHNOLOGY

In a major case designed to remove anticompetitive restraints imposed on American exports, the Division in May 1994 charged Pilkington, a British firm, and its U.S. subsidiary with monopolizing the flat glass market. The complaint alleged that Pilkington, which dominates the $15 billion a year international flat glass industry, foreclosed U.S. firms from foreign markets. Flat glass is used for windows and architectural panels by the construction industry and for windshields and windows by the automobile industry.

The Complaint alleged that Pilkington entered into unreasonably restrictive licensing arrangements with its most likely competitors, then over the course of almost three decades used these arrangements and threats of litigation to prevent American firms from competing to design, build and operate flat glass plants in other countries. By the time the Division filed its Complaint, Pilkington's patents had long since expired and its technology was in the public domain. A Consent Decree accepted by Pilkington to settle the case will bar it from restraining American and foreign firms who desire to sell their technology outside the United States. As a result, American firms will be able to compete for the 50 new glass plants expected to be built around the world over the next six years, resulting in an estimated increase in U.S. export revenues of as much as $1.25 billion during that period. This enforcement action builds on the Bush Administration's 1992 announcement that it would challenge such conduct and illustrates the Division's determination to address anticompetitive conduct that prevents

American firms from competing for business on fair terms in international markets.

FOUR: MILK AND DAIRY PRODUCTS CASES

As of September 30, 1994, the Division had filed 124 criminal cases against 73 corporations and 78 individuals in the milk and dairy products industry. To date, 63 corporations and 57 individuals have been convicted, and fines imposed total approximately $59 million. Twenty-seven individuals have been sentenced to serve a total of 4,774 days in jail, or an average of approximately 6 months. Civil damages assessed total approximately $8 million.

This sustained effort has broken up conspiracies that were illegally raising the price of milk supplied to children in public school districts across the country, including federally subsidized school lunch programs, as well as the price of dairy products supplied to the United States military. In FY 94, the division filed 18 criminal cases against 14 corporations and 11 individuals in the milk and dairy products industry. Seventeen grand juries in 14 states continue investigations in this industry.

FIVE: CELLULAR COMMUNICATIONS

In July 1994, the Division challenged the proposed acquisition by AT&T of McCaw Cellular, the nation's largest cellular telephone carrier, because this vertical merger could have raised prices and chilled innovation in cellular telephone services. These competitive concerns were addressed in a Consent Decree under which

☐ long-distance rivals of AT&T will have access to McCaw systems equal to AT&T's access;

☐ cellular rivals of McCaw that use AT&T equipment will continue to have access to necessary products and will be free of interference from AT&T should they wish to change equipment suppliers; and

☐ AT&T and McCaw will not misuse confidential information obtained from AT&T equipment customers or McCaw equipment suppliers.

The Consent Decree allows the parties to seek the potential benefits of integration in cellular services but prevents abuse of their economic power in the cellular services, cellular long distance and telecommunications equipment markets.

SIX: PERSONAL COMPUTER OPERATING SYSTEMS

The Division in July 1994 charged Microsoft, the world's largest computer software company, with violating the antimonopoly provisions of Section 2 of the Sherman Act. Microsoft licensed its MS-DOS and Windows technology on a "per processor" basis that required personal computer manufacturers to pay a fee to Microsoft for each computer shipped, even if the computer did not contain Microsoft's software. Microsoft's dominant position in the market induced many personal computer manufacturers to accept these per processor contracts, which penalized the manufacturers if they dealt with Microsoft's competitors. The Division's Complaint further alleged that Microsoft's licensing contracts bound computer manufacturers to the contracts for an unreasonably long period of time. As a result of these practices, the ability of rival operating systems to compete was impaired, innovation was slowed and consumer choice was limited. Microsoft also imposed overly restrictive nondisclosure agreements on software companies that participated in trial testing of new software, thereby impeding the ability of those firms to work with Microsoft's operating system rivals.

Microsoft agreed to accept a Consent Decree that enjoins these and other restrictive practices, and the Decree was filed along with the Division's Complaint. The tentative settlement was reached in close cooperation with the competition enforcement authorities of the European Commission, which had been investigating Microsoft's conduct since mid-1993, and marked the first coordinated effort of the two enforcement bodies in initiating and settling an antitrust case.

SEVEN: DEPARTMENT OF DEFENSE PROCUREMENT

The division challenged as an unreasonable restraint on competition a "teaming arrangement" between Alliant Techsystems and Aerojet-General to supply the Department of Defense with cluster bombs. The two defendants are the only two U.S. suppliers of cluster bombs, and their agreement not to compete on the DOD contract raised the price of the bombs substantially. The Division negotiated a resolution that recoups $12 million for taxpayers on DOD's 1992 procurement—about a ten percent savings. The case stemmed from coordinated efforts by the Departments of Defense and Justice. The Departments have worked to formalize their cooperation on competition policy in the defense industry based on the recommendations of the Defense Services Board Task Force on Defense Mergers, an interagency working group in which the Division participated . . .

EIGHT: COLLEGES

During the prior Administration, the Division charged that the Ivy League universities and MIT had conspired to fix the prices that financial aid applicants paid to attend those schools. The government alleged that the defendants met regularly to avoid competing against each other in the amount of financial aid—that is, tuition discounts—offered to applicants. The Ivy League schools entered into a Consent Decree that prohibited such agreements. MIT chose to litigate the matter. After a trial in 1992, the district court ruled that MIT had violated the antitrust laws. The Court of Appeals for the Third Circuit subsequently remanded the case for further analysis.

In December 1993, the Division and MIT settled the case when MIT agreed to abide by certain standards of conduct in the future. Those standards allow MIT to agree on general principles for determining financial aid with other colleges that adhere to a need-blind admissions policy and that award students financial aid to meet their full needs. Under the standards, colleges may not agree on the amount or composition of aid offered to individual applicants, on tuition rates or on faculty salaries. In October 1994, Congress enacted legislation that allows colleges following need-blind admissions policies only a more limited form of cooperation on financial aid matters than were set forth in the MIT standards of conduct.

Microsoft Back in the Dock

THE *NEW YORK TIMES**

Judge Stanley Sporkin has every right to feel frustrated. After four years of Federal investigation, the Justice Department and the Microsoft Corporation reached an antitrust settlement designed to end unfair, anticompetitive practices by the software giant. But neither Judge Sporkin nor any other outsider has the foggiest idea whether the agreement is adequate or a mere wrist slap when stronger measures are needed.

We still don't know whether Microsoft for the most part competes fairly, in which case it is a crown jewel of the American economy, just the sort of technological and business success this nation badly needs to compete in world markets in the coming information age. Or is Microsoft a predator that uses its market dominance to freeze out the superior products of competitors while insuring success for clunkier products of its own?

Microsoft is clearly the dominant powerhouse in providing software for personal computers. It manufactures the basic operating system (MS-DOS) that runs more than 70 percent of all personal computers. It produces Windows, a software program that allows users to manage scores of specialized applications programs. It also produces a powerful array of those applications programs itself, including a huge chunk of the word processors and spreadsheets used in personal computers.

*This editorial appeared in the *New York Times* on February 20, 1995.

80

The company's future plans are breathtaking. It hopes to develop its own on-line network and seeks to purchase a company whose personal-finance software dominates that market, opening the way for electronic banking and purchasing.

But as Microsoft has become ever more dominant, complaints about its practices have mounted. The Federal Government has investigated Microsoft for the past four years, first at the Federal Trade Commission, inconclusively, then at the Justice Department, where Assistant Attorney General Anne K. Bingaman has been trying to revive the antitrust division from its torpor during the Reagan-Bush years. Last July, the long Federal probe reached an anticlimactic conclusion—a narrow consent decree in which Microsoft agreed to change certain licensing practices that seem clearly anticompetitive.

For example, Microsoft had been requiring computer manufacturers who licensed its MS-DOS operating system to pay a royalty for every computer they sold, even if many of those computers did not actually use MS-DOS but contained a rival operating system instead. That put enormous pressure on the manufacturers to shun the rival system altogether. Microsoft has now agreed to abandon the practice, and to stop a few other licensing practices also deemed unfair.

That's a clear gain. But Judge Sporkin, who must rule whether the decree is in the public interest, rejected it last week for failing to address critical issues. The judge complained that, even on the licensing practices, the agreement would simply require Microsoft to "sin no more." It would do nothing to offset the unfair advantage Microsoft had already gained. He is unquestionably right on this point; the only issue is what can be done about it.

Even more important, Judge Sporkin expressed concern that Justice may have caved in on some very big issues that the consent decree does not even address. For example, there are complaints that Microsoft has an intimidating habit of announcing, prematurely, that a new product will be coming out so that customers will not buy a competitive product. Others accuse Microsoft of using its dominant position in operating systems to give its own applications designers an advantage over rival software designers. The judge was particularly frustrated by the Justice Department's refusal to say what practices it had investigated and what findings it made before letting issues drop.

Both Justice and Microsoft are appealing to a higher court, contending that Judge Sporkin exceeded his authority. Justice claims its ability to negotiate consent decrees would be crippled if judges can wade in after the fact and demand that other issues be addressed and investigative findings be revealed. But control of the electronics marketplace is too important to be settled in secret. The public needs full disclosure from Justice to make certain that this fabulously successful company is behaving properly and not setting up roadblocks on the emerging information highway.

QUESTIONS FOR ANALYSIS

1. According to Assistant Attorney General Bingaman, the "fundamental thesis of strong antitrust enforcement is that rivalry, not market power, fosters innovation and efficiency over the long run." What evidence does she provide in support of this thesis?

2. Ms. Bingaman argues that an "effective antitrust enforcement program promotes innovation by . . . reducing barriers to entry." Why? Does the Pilkington case illustrate this point? If so, how?

3. She also says that the "arguments of those who endorse collaborative research and the development of national champions as the generally preferred method of advancement find little support in recent developments." What recent developments does she have in mind?

4. A central point of Ms. Bingaman's speech is that "innovation is critically important to the advancement of this nation's economic interests." Do you agree? Why or why not?

5. Does she argue that the government has no role in the innovative process? If not, what role does she regard as appropriate?

6. According to the Antitrust Division, an international cartel fixed prices in the thermal fax paper market. Why is this against the law?

7. The Antitrust Division challenged as an unreasonable restraint on competition a "teaming arrangement" between Alliant Techsystems and Aerojet-General to supply the Department of Defense with cluster bombs. Why?

8. According to Ms. Bingaman, "the proposed *Microsoft* consent decree does precisely what the antitrust laws are designed to do: provide a level playing field so that all competitors have a fair shot at success on the merits." But Judge Stanley Sporkin rejected the agreement between Microsoft and the Justice Department. Why?

9. What complaints have been made about Microsoft's practices?

10. The *New York Times* complains that "We still don't know whether Microsoft for the most part competes fairly . . . Or is Microsoft a predator . . . ?" How can this issue be resolved? What sorts of evidence are relevant? What would convince you one way or the other?

PART FIVE

THE ENVIRON-

MENT

Many people, including distinguished scientists and leading statesmen and stateswomen, are worried about what is happening to the environment; others feel that economic growth is being curtailed unnecessarily by alarmists who exaggerate the environmental risks. The first article, by Lester R. Brown of Worldwatch Institute, argues that our generation will be judged by whether we can reverse the environmental degradation of the planet. The second article, by President Clinton's Council of Economic Advisers, describes some of the environmental policies of the Clinton administration.

A New Era Unfolds

LESTER R. BROWN*

In early 1992, the U.S. National Academy of Sciences and the Royal Society of London issued a joint report that began: "If current predictions of population growth prove accurate and patterns of human activity on the planet remain unchanged, science and technology may not be able to prevent either irreversible degradation of the environment or continued poverty for much of the world."

It was a remarkable statement—an admission that science and technology can no longer ensure a better future unless population growth slows quickly and the economy is restructured. This abandonment of the technological optimism by two of the world's leading scientific bodies represents a major, though perhaps not surprising, shift—given the deteriorating state of the planet. A deepening concern about the future among scientists is indicated by their first-ever joint statement.

Despite the intensifying global interest in the planet's future, the U.N. conference on Environment and Development, convened last June in Rio de Janeiro, fell short of both hopes and expectations. Many of the difficulties centered on the U.S. insistence that goals and timetables for restricting carbon emissions be removed from the climate treaty, leaving it little more than a statement of good intentions. The convention designed to protect

*Lester R. Brown is president of Worldwatch Institute. This article appeared in *Challenge*, May/June 1993.

biological diversity had some flaws, but perhaps the most serious one was the missing U.S. signature. Yet, it was not a total loss by any means. The climate treaty, which was signed by 154 participating countries (including the United States), recognizes that global warming is a serious issue. And it does provide for setting up an international system for governments to report each year on changes in carbon emissions. This information flow itself will focus attention on the threat of climate change.

FLAWED ACCOUNTING SYSTEMS

The Rio conference presented an opportunity for taking stock of environmental gains and losses. Individual countries presented national state-of-the-environment reports, typically emphasizing their achievements. The descriptions included countless examples of local gains in achieving cleaner air and water, greater recycling of materials, and reforestation. These improvements notwithstanding, the broad indicators showed a continuing wholesale deterioration in the earth's physical condition. Since 1972, farmers have lost nearly 500 billion tons of topsoil through erosion—at a time when they were called on to feed 1.6 billion additional people. Atmospheric concentrations of carbon dioxide (CO_2), the principal greenhouse gas, climbed 9 percent. The risks to life on earth posed by the loss of stratospheric ozone and the associated increase of ultraviolet radiation—a threat not even imagined in 1972—were on everyone's mind.

These environmental concerns exist, in part, because of a misleading economic accounting system and a largely nonexistent biological accounting system. The internationally accepted system of national economic accounting used to calculate gross national product (GNP) rightly subtracts the depreciation of plant and equipment from the overall output of goods and services; but it takes no account of the depreciation of natural capital—such as the loss of topsoil from erosion, the destruction of forests by acid rain, or the depletion of the protective stratospheric ozone layer. As a result, the economic accounting system now used by governments greatly overstates progress. Failing to reflect reality, it generates environmentally destructive economic policies and is fragmentary at best.

No one knows how many species of plants and animals are lost each year, indeed, lacking a global inventory of the earth's biological resources, no one even knows how many species there are. Visual evidence from occasional national surveys and satellite data tell us that forests are disappearing in many countries. Similarly, incomplete data indicate that grasslands are deteriorating. Closely associated with the reduced grass and tree cover is the loss of topsoil. Despite the essential economic role of soil, no global data-gathering system measures its gains or losses. Nor does the biological accounting system warn when carrying-capacity thresholds are crossed. We learn that cattle numbers are excessive only when the rangeland begins to deteriorate. We discover that demands on forests are excessive only when they begin to disappear. We find that we have been overfishing only when the catch drops precipitously. Lacking information on sustainable yields, governments have permitted demands on these natural systems to become excessive, leading to their gradual destruction.

The result of this flawed economic accounting system and largely nonexistent biological accounting system is widespread degradation and destruction of the economy's environmental support-systems. Industrial firms are allowed to internalize profits while externalizing costs, passing on to society such expenses as those for health care associated with polluted air or those arising from global warming.

We can expect an expanding economy based on such an incomplete accounting system to slowly undermine itself, eventually collapsing as support-systems are destroyed. And that is *just* what is happening. The environmentally destructive activities of recent decades are now showing up in:

☐ reduced productivity of croplands, forests, grasslands, and fisheries;

☐ the mounting cleanup costs of toxic waste sites;

☐ rising health-care costs for cancer, birth defects, allergies, emphysema, asthma, and other respiratory diseases;

☐ the spread of hunger.

Rapid population growth, environmental degradation, and deepening poverty are reinforcing each other in a downward spiral in many countries. In its *World Development Report 1992*, the World Bank reported that per capita GNP had fallen in 49 countries during the eighties. Almost all these nations, containing 846 million people, are low-income, largely agrarian economies experiencing rapid population growth and extensive degradation of their forests, grasslands, and croplands. As the Royal Society/National Academy statement implies, it may not be possible to reverse this fall in living standards of nearly one-sixth of humanity if rapid population growth continues and existing patterns of economic activity are not changed. Just how difficult it will be is only now becoming clear. There is also a real risk that the demographic pressures and environmental deterioration that are replacing progress with decline will spread, enveloping even more of humanity during the nineties.

THE ECONOMIC COSTS

Many people have long understood, at least intuitively, that continuing environmental degradation would eventually exact a heavy economic toll. Unfortunately, no global economic models incorporate the depletion and destruction of the earth's natural support-systems. Only now can we begin to piece together information from several recent independent studies to get a sense of the worldwide economic effects of environmental degradation. Among the most revealing of these are studies on the effects of:

☐ air pollution and acid rain on forests in Europe;

☐ land degradation on livestock and crop production in the world's dryland regions;

☐ global warming on the U.S. economy;

☐ pollution on health in Russia.

These reports and other data show that the fivefold growth in the world economy since 1950 and the increase in population from 2.6 billion to 5.5 billion have begun to outstrip the carrying capacity of biological support-systems and the ability of natural systems to absorb waste without being damaged. In country after country, demands for crops and for the products of grasslands, forests, and fisheries are exceeding the sustainable yield of these systems. Once this happens, the resource itself begins to shrink as natural capital is consumed. Overstocking grasslands, overcutting forests, overplowing, and overfishing are now commonplace. Every country is practicing the environmental equivalent of deficit financing in one form or another. . . .

THE END OF RAPID GNP GROWTH

As noted earlier, our existing economic accounting system makes it difficult to assess the effect on the economy of both environmental degradation and the inherent constraints imposed by the carrying capacity of natural systems. We know that they will constrain future expansion of food and other essential commodities, but we do not know how much. Until we have an accounting system that incorporates natural-capital depreciation and losses, we cannot measure progress or decline accurately. For the time being, then, policymakers are forced to rely on GNP, which overstates progress.

More and more evidence indicates that the productivity of the earth's biological systems is emerging as a constraint on the growth of the economy and ultimately on that of population. This is most evident in the Third World, where the falling productivity of forests, grasslands, and, in some countries, croplands is reducing living standards.

In scores of developing countries, per capita grain production has been falling far longer than it has for the world as a whole. In Africa, the decline has been under way since 1970, dropping an average of roughly 1 percent a year. Such a decrease in a largely agrarian society is often followed by a decline in per capita GNP. Indeed, of the 49 countries where per capita GNP fell during the eighties, the great majority had experienced a drop in per capita-grain production. Globally, if growth in grain output cannot be raised from the 1 percent annually of the last several years to something close to the 3 percent a year that was helping eradicate hunger from mid-century until 1984, slow agricultural growth will become a severe constraint on world economic growth.

The production of beef and mutton on grasslands is also pushing against nature's boundaries. With rare exceptions, the world's grasslands are now either fully used or overused; in many areas they cannot sustain even the present output. A study of rangeland productivity in Pakistan's semiarid regions reports that overgrazing has reduced productivity to 15 to 40 percent of its potential. It describes the livestock sector as "caught in a downward spiral of too many sick animals chasing too little feed." Yet, putting more cattle and sheep in feedlots and expanding fish farming require more grain and soybean meal, further intensifying the competition with humans for grain.

As to forests, the demand for firewood and lumber exceeds forest regeneration by a wide margin in China, the Indian subcontinent, and semiarid Africa—areas that contain nearly half of humanity. Many developing countries that once exported forest products—such as Nigeri—are now importers. Of the 33 remaining Third World exporters of forest products, only 10 are projected to remain in that position by the end of this decade. With productive forests shrinking, the prospect for rapid long-term expansion of this sector is not good.

Agriculture also supplies industrial raw materials. Farms and forests together supply cotton and wool for the textile industries, leather for the leather goods industries, lumber for construction, wood pulp for paper, and many other basic inputs. Indeed, with the important exceptions of minerals and petrochemical products, virtually all the raw materials used in industry are of biological origin, coming from the agricultural and forestry sectors. Slower growth in world farm output thus affects not only the food prospect but the industrial growth prospect as well.

In addition to the constraints imposed by the maximum sustainable yield of forests, grasslands, and fisheries, the amount of fresh water produced by the hydrological cycle is impairing economic expansion in many countries. In more and more locations, the threefold growth in world water use since mid-century is pushing demand beyond the amount the hydrological cycle can supply. Water scarcity and falling water tables are now commonplace in the former Soviet Asian republics, the Middle East, North China, parts of India, North Africa, parts of sub-Saharan Africa, and the southwestern United States.

Pollution-cleanup costs are siphoning public capital away from investment in education, health care, and other key needs. Societies everywhere are facing huge cleanup costs for toxic chemical waste sites and areas contaminated with nuclear radiation. In some countries the costs have risen to billions of dollars; in larger industrial economies, such as the United States, they've surged to hundreds of billions.

The costs of environmentally induced illnesses, both those of health care and lost labor productivity, are mounting everywhere. We are only beginning to feel the effects. These illnesses cause an enormous drain on the financial resources of societies, and will take a heavy toll on labor-force productivity.

DECLINING GLOBAL GROWTH

Even a cursory glance at global economic growth, decade by decade, since mid-century shows the emergence of a disturbing trend for the world's poor (see Table 2). World economic growth exceeded that of population

TABLE 2   World Economic Growth by Decade, 1950–92

DECADE	ANNUAL GROWTH OF WORLD ECONOMY	ANNUAL GROWTH PER PERSON
1950–60	4.9%	3.1%
1960–70	5.2%	3.2%
1970–80	3.4%	1.6%
1980–90	2.9%	1.1%
1990–92	0.6%	−1.1%

Sources: World Bank, Department of Socio-Economic Data, unpublished printout, February 1992; International Monetary Fund, *World Economic Outlook,* October 1992; World Product in 1950 from Herbert R. Block; *The Planetary Product in 1980: A Creative Pause?,* U.S. Department of State, 1981; Population data from PRB, *World Population Data Sheets.*

by more than 3 percent during the fifties and sixties, providing a substantial gain in living standards for much of humanity. This was roughly cut in half during the seventies; it dropped even further during the eighties. And the nineties are not off to a good start. As a result of the global recession, per capita income fell by over 2 percent from 1990 to 1992. Even with a strong rebound, it could be mid-decade before incomes regain their 1990 level, giving the world five years with no improvement in living standards.

Now directly affecting national and global economic trends, environmental degradation can no longer be considered a peripheral issue. If destruction of the economy's support-systems continues, growth in economic output could fall below that of population, pulling average incomes down for the entire world. The world is entering a new era, one in which future economic progress depends on reversing environmental degradation. This, in turn, is contingent on new economic and population policies.

A NEW WORLD

It is evident that the existing economic system is slowly beginning to self-destruct as it undermines its environmental support-systems. The challenge is to design and build an economic system that is environmentally sustainable. Can we envision what this would look like? Can we devise a strategy for getting from here to there in the time that is available? The answer is "yes" to both questions.

The basic components of an effort to build an environmentally sustainable global economy are rather straightforward. They include:

☐ re-establishing climate stability;

☐ protecting the stratospheric ozone layer;

☐ restoring the earth's tree cover;

☐ stabilizing soils;

☐ safeguarding the earth's remaining biological diversity;

☐ restoring the traditional balance between births and deaths.

The future is replete with opportunities to reverse our current course:

☐ Traditional incandescent light bulbs, for example, would be replaced by the latest compact fluorescents, providing the same light but using only one-quarter as much electricity.

□ Solar energy is the only viable option to fossil fuels. It takes many forms: hydropower (already supplying one-fifth of the world's electricity), wind power, solar thermal power plants, firewood, photovoltaic cells, agricultural wastes, rooftop solar water heaters, alcohol fuels from sugar cane, and many more. All are likely to play a role.

□ The costs of photovoltaic cells are coming down fast; they are likely to play an important role eventually. The latest of these converts a phenomenal 22 percent of sunlight into electricity and produces it for 8¢ per kilowatt hour, well below the 12¢ for electricity from new nuclear plants in the state, but still above the 6¢ for that from coal-fired plants.

□ As costs continue to drop, the resulting cheap solar electricity permits the production of hydrogen fuel from the simple electrolysis of water. Hydrogen provides a means of both storing solar energy and transporting it efficiently over long distances, either by pipeline or by tanker, in much the same way that natural gas is transported.

□ Natural gas can serve as a bridging fuel, linking the fossil fuel era with the solar age. Shifting from coal or oil to natural gas sharply reduces air pollution and carbon emissions per unit of energy produced. And the facilities and pipelines now used to store and transport natural gas can one day be used for hydrogen.

□ There is a new awareness of the threat of unbridled population growth. Relating future population growth to the availability of cropland, fresh water, forest products, and grazing area along with the need for classrooms, health care, and jobs can serve as a guide to responsible policies.

One of the great tragedies of the last decade has been the withdrawal of all U.S. financial support for the U.N. Population Fund and the International Planned Parenthood Federation—the two principal agencies engaged in family planning internationally. This is one reason that up to 300 million of the world's women do not yet have access to family-planning services. Demographic surveys indicate that one in four births in the Third World is unplanned and unwanted. This fact explains, in part, the millions of street children there. Simply eliminating unwanted births would cut world population growth by more than one-third.

Glimpses of what our new world would look like can be seen here and there:

□ Japan has set the international standard for energy efficiency and, in the process, strengthened its competitive position in world markets.

☐ California, with its rapidly growing solar and wind industries, provides a window on future energy sources. Its solar thermal electric generating capacity of 350 megawatts and its wind generating capacity of 1,600 megawatts are enough to satisfy the residential needs of nearly 2 million people, easily enough for San Francisco, San Diego, and Sacramento combined.

☐ Thailand has halved its growth rate in less than 15 years.

☐ In the effort to stabilize soils, the United States' innovative Conservation Reserve Program (adopted in 1985) reduced soil erosion by one-third by 1990, and may cut it by another one-third by 1995.

☐ Germany has instituted a comprehensive program designed to force companies to assume responsibility for disposing of the packaging used with their products. Denmark has gone even further—banning unrefillable beverage containers.

In the end, we need not merely a vision, but a shared vision, one that guides and unites us in our day-to-day decision-making. Such a vision—a common blueprint—can infuse society with a sense of purpose as we try to build a new world, one much more attractive than today's. This sense of common purpose and excitement is essential if we are to create an environmentally sustainable economic system.

FACING UP TO CHANGE

The deterioration in living conditions for much of humanity during the eighties and early nineties will continue if economies are not restructured. It is in the largely agrarian economies that the link between deteriorating natural systems and living conditions is most direct, and the effects most visible.

At some point, the costs of deteriorating forests, dying lakes, damaged crops, respiratory illnesses, increasing temperatures, rising sea level, and other effects of fossil-fuel use become unacceptably high. Basic economics argues for a switch to solar energy. If the eventual consequence of failing to respond is catastrophe, the answer is obvious.

We are facing great change. There is little doubt of that. If we try to build the new economic system slowly, time will run out and environmental deterioration will lead to economic decline. The question is whether we will initiate the changes in time and manage the process, or whether the forces of deterioration and decline will prevail, acquiring a momentum of their own.

And since we have little experience in the modern era with which to judge it, we cannot be certain what the deterioration/decline scenario would look like.

The challenge is not only about what we need to do, but how we can do it quickly—before time runs out and the entire world is caught in the downward spiral that already has roughly one-sixth of humanity in its grip. Among the principal policy instruments that can convert a slowly self-destructing economic system into one that is environmentally sustainable are regulations and tax policy. Until now, governments have relied heavily on regulation, but the record of the last two decades shows that this is not a winning strategy.

Regulations clearly do have some role to play. They are needed in the handling of toxic waste and radioactive materials—things too dangerous to leave to the marketplace. Environmentally damaging chemicals, such as CFCs, can be banned. Energy efficiency standards for automobiles and household appliances can cut carbon emissions, air pollution, and acid rain.

By far the most effective instrument to transform the economy quickly, however, is tax policy, specifically the partial replacement of income taxes with environmental taxes. And tax policy permits the market to work unimpeded, preserving its inherent efficiency. Today, governments tax income because it is an easy way to collect revenue, even though it serves no particular social purpose. Replacing a portion of income taxes with environmental taxes would help to transform the economy quickly. This shift would encourage work and savings and would discourage environmentally destructive activities. In short, it would foster productive activities and discourage destructive ones, guiding both corporate investments and consumer expenditures.

Among the activities that ought to be taxed are the burning of fossil fuels, the production of hazardous chemical waste, the generation of nuclear waste, pesticide use, and the use of virgin raw materials. The adoption of a carbon tax, which would discourage the burning of fossil fuels, is now being actively considered in both the European Community and Japan. Even a modest carbon tax would quickly tip the scales away from investment in fossil-fuel production and toward investment in energy efficiency and renewable energy sources. Within a year of adoption of an international carbon tax, literally scores of solar thermal plants could be under construction.

The measure of individuals or nations is whether they respond to the great issues of their time. For our generation, the great issues are environment and poverty. We will be judged by whether we can reverse the environmental degradation of the planet and eradicate the dehumanizing poverty that is now engulfing more and more of the world's people.

We know what we have to do. And we know how to do it. If we fail to convert our self-destructing economy into one that is environmentally sustainable, future generations will be overwhelmed by environmental degradation and social disintegration.

Simply stated, if our generation does not turn things around, our children may not have the option of doing so.

Addressing Environmental Externalities

Joseph E. Stiglitz

PRESIDENT CLINTON'S COUNCIL OF ECONOMIC ADVISERS*

T he notion of tradeoffs is among the most fundamental in economics: nothing is free; everything has an opportunity cost. In private markets, tradeoffs are handled automatically, as consumers choose among alternative goods and services and producers choose among alternative inputs. Prices guide these decisions. Tradeoffs involving the environment cannot be made so easily, however, because use of the environment is generally unpriced. As a result, firms and individuals, in their marketplace decisions, do not always make the best tradeoffs from the standpoint of society as a whole. The effects of failing to price environmental goods and services are examples of externalities (Box 7). When externalities are significant, the government can often design policies that improve the functioning of markets and thereby increase aggregate social welfare.

The Administration has sought to encourage the development of environmental technologies to mitigate tradeoffs and foster economic growth. Improvements in the technologies for preventing and treating pollution, and efforts to spread knowledge about technologies already available, can free resources for other socially beneficial purposes or permit the attainment of higher environmental goals without increasing the burden on the economy. Given the worldwide explosion in environmental regulatory ac-

*This is an excerpt from the *Economic Report of the President* (Washington, DC: Government Printing Office, 1994).

96

BOX 7. **EXTERNALITIES**

An externality, or spillover, is a type of market failure that arises when the private costs or benefits of production differ from the social costs or benefits. For example, if a factory pollutes, and neither the firm nor its customers pay for the harm that pollution causes, the pollution is an externality. In the presence of this negative (harmful) externality, market forces will generate too much of the activity causing the externality, here the factory's production, and too much of the externality itself, here the pollution. In the case of beneficial externalities, firms will generate too little of the activity causing the externality, and too little of the externality itself, because they are not compensated for the benefits they offer. For example, the development of laser technology has had beneficial effects far beyond whatever gains its developers captured, improving products in industries as diverse as medicine and telecommunications. Too little research and development and other activities generating positive externalities will take place in the absence of some governmental intervention.

To remedy market failures and induce the market to provide the efficient level of the externality-causing activity, the private parties involved in the activity must face the full social costs and benefits of their actions. Policymakers may employ a variety of tools to accomplish this result, such as taxes, user fees, subsidies, or the establishment or clarification of property rights.

---

tivity—in the Far East, in eastern Europe, in Mexico, and elsewhere—the development of more effective and lower cost pollution control technology can also increase our export competitiveness. In fact, we already enjoy considerable success in this area. The United States is now the world leader in exports of environmental equipment. In a global market for environmental technologies of $295 billion in 1992, the $134 billion U.S. share is the largest by far. Our trade surplus in pollution control equipment has been increasing and was $1.1 billion in 1991.

The Administration has also sought to improve the "technology" of regulating the use of natural and environmental resources. This effort involves seeking a better balance among conflicting interests in the use of natural resources, and developing approaches to regulate pollution that rely more on economic incentives and eliminate the economic distortions of some current regulations. Examples of improving the technology for regulating the environment are found in the Administration's plan for managing the old growth forests of the Pacific Northwest, in its approach to grazing on Federal lands, in the Climate Change Action Plan, and in the Administration's position favoring the reauthorization of the Comprehensive Environmental Response, Compensation, and Liability Act, better known as

"Superfund." To better assess where interventions to improve the environment will benefit the economy, the Administration is also engaged in efforts to define sustainable development and develop "green" GDP accounts.

MANAGING RESOURCES ON FEDERAL LANDS

The Federal Government owns vast tracts of land, primarily in the West. These lands contain natural resources of economic importance to both local communities and the Nation, including timber and other forest products, forage for grazing livestock, and mineral deposits. They are also sources of extremely valuable environmental amenities, such as open space for recreational uses like wildlife viewing, scenery, camping, hiking, and hunting; fish and wildlife (including endangered species) habitat; watershed protection; and many others.

Improving the "technology" of regulating the use of these Federal lands is a centerpiece of Administration policy. Two principles guide that policy: (1) reducing inefficiencies caused by improper pricing and regulatory restrictions, and (2) ensuring that both pricing and regulation will achieve a better balance among competing uses of these resources, particularly between extractive (timber, grazing, mining) and environmental uses. These principles can be seen at work in the Administration's plans for managing old growth forests in the Pacific Northwest and for rangeland reform.

Old Growth Forests, Spotted Owls, and Timber

The controversy over logging in the old growth forests and spotted owl habitat of the Northwest provides a case study in reconciling environmental and economic objectives and illustrates how a careful balancing of competing interests can result in progress on all fronts.

The forest products industry is a major industry in the Pacific Northwest, where it is heavily dependent on timber from Federal lands. Much of the Federal land on which this logging has taken place consists of mature forest stands. Referred to as "old growth," this mature forest is the habitat of the northern spotted owl, a threatened species, and many other plants and animals.

For several years Federal forest policy in the Northwest failed to take appropriate account of impacts on environmental quality and biodiversity. In particular, timber harvests on Federal lands were accelerated substantially in the mid- and late 1980s: Such harvests in the habitat of the spotted owl rose from 2.4 billion board feet (bbf) in 1982 to 6.7 bbf in 1988. According to experts, these levels were too high to be sustained indefinitely. Legal challenges to Federal timber policy resulted in injunctions blocking the sale of timber on Federal forest lands in the spotted owl region, in part be-

cause agencies within the Federal Government had failed to work coopera-
tively to comply with environmental and forest management laws. The injunctions had a severe impact on the timber industry, albeit in large part
because harvest levels had been extraordinarily and unsustainably large.

The Administration put a high priority on resolving the problems associated with forest management policy in the Pacific Northwest. Accordingly,
in July 1993, the Administration announced a "Forest Plan for a Sustainable Economy and a Sustainable Environment." The plan attempts to end
the uncertainty caused by legal wrangling and confusion and ameliorate
the impact of economic dislocation, while achieving full compliance with
existing laws. It also seeks to maintain and improve the ecosystem as a
whole, balance the interests of competing uses of the ecosystem for environmental and economic purposes, and create a political consensus to
avoid economic instability.

The plan provides for the maximum legally defensible harvest from Federal forests in the spotted owl region (about 1.2 bbf annually). The process
of adjustment to the new, lower harvest levels will be smoothed by an economic adjustment plan that is expected to create more than 8,000 new jobs
and 5,400 retraining opportunities in the region in 1994. Many of the new
jobs will be in enterprises that improve water quality, expand the prospects
for commercial fishing, and improve forest management in the region.

The plan focuses on maintaining and improving the environmental quality of watersheds in the region, recognizing how the complex interactions
of flora, fauna, and human activities affect that ecosystem. It establishes old
growth reserves and protects over 6.5 million acres of old growth forest
(about 80 percent of existing old growth). It also establishes 10 "adaptive
management areas" for experimentation into better ways of integrating
ecological and economic objectives.

Rangeland Reform

The Federal Government owns extensive rangelands throughout the West.
While these lands are used primarily for grazing cattle and sheep, increased demand for environmental uses has fueled controversy over Federal management. The controversy over rangeland reform shows the
importance of integrating pricing with regulation to use the Nation's resources more efficiently and strike a better balance between economic and
environmental objectives.

A central point of contention involves the fees that the Federal Government charges ranchers to graze animals on Federal land. These fees should
reflect both the value of the forage used by an additional animal and the
external environmental costs of grazing an additional animal (such as
the value of reductions in recreation or water quality). Charging ranchers

the marginal value of forage, the first component, encourages efficient use of the range. By preventing overgrazing, it protects the condition of the range for future grazing uses. It also promotes long-run efficiency in the livestock industry: Prices for forage that are too low encourage excessive investment in the industry. Forage value varies from tract to tract because of differences in forage productivity, location, proximity to roads and other transportation, rainfall, and access to water. But it can still be measured easily and reliably using the value of private rangelands in nearby locations. The second component, the external costs of grazing, cannot be determined from private market transactions. But economists have developed ways of inferring the value of open space or other environmental amenities from the costs people willingly incur to use them or from sophisticated survey methods.

Current Federal management policies are relics of an earlier era when the Federal Government used resource subsidies to encourage settlement of the West. One result is that grazing fees on Federal lands average only 17 to 37 percent of the value of grazing on comparable private lands. Moreover, the formula used to calculate Federal grazing fees has kept those fees from increasing along with private grazing lease rates. Promoting efficiency thus means both increasing grazing fees and ensuring that Federal grazing fees change from year to year in accordance with changes in rent on private grazing land. The Administration's plans for rangeland reform do both. The current proposal calls for phasing in a new fee structure that more than doubles current fees, and for using an updating formula that will adjust Federal fees at the same rate that private fees change.

Pricing reform must be accompanied by changes in regulation. For example, Federal grazing permits have "use-it-or-lose-it" provisions, under which decreases in the number of animals grazed may result in the loss of a grazing permit or a reduction in the number of animals that the permitholder may graze in the future. This policy prevents ranchers from temporarily reducing the number of animals grazed to improve range condition. The Administration's plan allows the terms of grazing permits to be rewritten to allow ranchers to vary the number of animals they graze in response to changes in weather or economic conditions. The plan also includes provisions to strengthen environmental management.

CLIMATE CHANGE ACTION PLAN

Certain gases emitted into the atmosphere by industrial, automotive, and other combustion have been implicated as a threat to the global climate: By preventing reflected solar radiation from escaping into space, these "greenhouse gases" may be causing a generalized warming of the planet. For this reason, an international agreement to reduce greenhouse gas emissions, the Framework Convention on Climate Change, was signed in 1992. The previous Administration had adopted what was called a "no regrets" policy; it was willing to take steps to reduce emissions only if those actions would be beneficial for other reasons—that is, even if greenhouse gas emissions were ultimately found unrelated to changes in the global climate. In contrast, this Administration sees cost-effective policies to reduce greenhouse gas emissions as appropriate "insurance" against the threat of climate change. Accordingly, the President, in his Earth Day speech on April 21, 1993, issued a "clarion call" for the creation of a cost-effective plan to reduce U.S. greenhouse gas emissions to 1990 levels by the year 2000.

The President's call resulted 6 months later in the Climate Change Action Plan, containing nearly 50 initiatives that cover reductions in all significant greenhouse gases and will affect most sectors of the economy. The plan was based on the understanding that the climate change threat results from *all* greenhouse gases, that it depends on *net* emissions (after accounting for greenhouse gas "sinks" such as forests and oceans), and that the problem is *global.* The strategies adopted to address the externalities associated with greenhouse gas emissions were chosen on the basis of a qualitative assessment of the cost-effectiveness of the alternatives, in part by selecting policies that make markets work better.

Some of the strategies expand upon initiatives of this and previous Administrations to promote energy-saving technology. For example, the Green Lights program improves the diffusion of technology by providing consumers and firms with information about environmentally friendly products such as energy-saving lights that promise to reduce electricity generation and the resulting emissions. Other strategies reduce emissions by making government more efficient. Two examples are (1) reform of regulations that block the seasonal use of natural gas (a low-polluting alternative to coal) by electric utilities, and (2) removal of regulatory impediments to private investments in upgrading Federal hydroelectric facilities.

Parking Cashout

Greenhouse gas emissions will also be reduced by improving the pricing of activities that generate externalities. The parking cashout policy attempts to correct a distortion in private incentives resulting from the tax treatment of employer-provided parking. Currently, the Internal Revenue Code allows employers to deduct any costs for employer-provided parking as a business expense, and lets workers exclude the benefits from their taxable income (up to $155 a month). As a result, 95 percent of automobile commuters receive free or subsidized parking, more than half of them in central business districts. All told, U.S. companies claim $52 billion per year in parking-related deductions from this free or subsidized service.

The Climate Change Action Plan proposes that Federal tax laws be modified to require that firms offer employees the option of taking the cash value of their employer-provided parking benefit as taxable income rather than accepting their free parking space. The program would apply initially only to those firms with more than 25 employees that make monthly cash payments for their employees to park in lots owned by third parties. Thus, only about 15 percent of employer-provided parking would be covered at first, although the program would expand later as new parking leases are negotiated.

This policy change should reduce the overuse of automobiles for commuting resulting from the current parking subsidy, by making commuters face more of the social costs of driving. As consumers shift to carpools and public transportation, greenhouse gas emissions, other pollutants, and traffic congestion should all be reduced. Other distortions of the choice between commuting by car and by public transit will remain uncorrected, however, to the extent that current regulation of automobile emissions does not fully capture their environmental, congestion, and health costs.

International Strategies for Greenhouse Gas Reductions

One hundred and sixty-one countries signed the Framework Convention on Climate Change in 1992, agreeing that it is necessary to stabilize greenhouse gas concentrations at a level that will prevent "dangerous anthropogenic interference with the climate system." Because this is a global problem, the Climate Change Action Plan addressed what is termed "joint implementation"—the cooperative effort between countries or entities within them to reduce greenhouse gas emissions. The plan recognizes that there may be enormous cost savings to meeting global goals for greenhouse gas reductions if acceptable international strategies can be developed to reduce emissions where it is cheapest to do so, rather than have each country pursue its emissions reduction goals on its own. Some important questions need resolution, however, such as how reductions are to be identified, monitored, and enforced. To begin testing the joint implementation concept, the plan creates a pilot program that evaluates investments by U.S. firms and government assistance to foreign countries for new greenhouse gas emission reductions; measures, tracks, and scores these reductions; and, in general, lays a foundation for broader, more formal policy initiatives in the future.

SUPERFUND REAUTHORIZATION: THE ADMINISTRATION POSITION

The Comprehensive Environmental Response, Compensation, and Liability Act, better known as Superfund, was enacted in 1980 and amended in 1986 in response to widespread concerns that improperly disposed-of wastes threatened human health and valuable natural resources, such as groundwater aquifers. The act has been unsatisfactory in addressing this problem. Fewer than 20 percent of the 1,300 disposal sites on the priority list drawn up by the Environmental Protection Agency (EPA) have been fully "cleaned up," although 3,500 separate actions have been taken to remove wastes posing an immediate threat to health.

At the same time, the costs of the program have been substantial, running almost $7 billion per year. This figure includes direct draws on the Superfund trust fund collected from the oil and chemical industries to pay for EPA expenses (including $1.6 billion in spending on cleanups where no private parties can be assigned responsibility), $3.2 billion in spending by Federal agencies that own or contributed to hazardous waste sites, and $2 billion in spending by private parties, much of which goes to lawyers' fees and other transactions costs in an effort to escape or reduce liability. Some estimates put the total cost of cleaning up the 3,000 sites projected to be on the EPA's National Priority List (NPL) over the next 30 to 40 years at $130 billion to $150 billion, with $200 billion to $300 billion more needed for Federal facility cleanups.

In response to the poor cost-effectiveness and slow pace of this program, the Administration has proposed several significant reforms. The two most important involve the standards and processes governing the cleanup strategy chosen at a site, and the process for assigning and financing liability.

Remedy Selection

Under the current law, remedial measures at Superfund sites are chosen with a preference for treatment and permanent cleanup of soil and water. They are also selected to meet high standards of cleanliness: land generally must become suitable for residential use, and water often must achieve drinking quality. Costs have little weight in remedy selection; they come into play only to identify the cheapest of the set of remedies meeting other criteria.

The Administration's position establishes more reasonable goals and processes for cleanup decisions. It sets uniform national goals for health and environmental protection to guide remedy selection. It substitutes a concern for long-term reliability as a factor to consider in remedy selection, in place of the preference for treatment and permanence (except for treatment of "hot spots"). It explicitly recognizes containment as a legitimate cleanup strategy. It limits the use of State and Federal standards designed for other pollution contexts. Finally, it introduces greater flexibility and community input into the determination of appropriate land use for the site, permitting some sites to be designated for industrial use, with appropriately lower levels of cleanup required.

The Administration's proposal also offers a streamlined approach to remedy selection at individual sites. With EPA approval, parties will be able to avail themselves of a set of cost-effective "generic" remedies established by the EPA that apply to certain frequently encountered types of waste disposal problems. Alternatively, they can formulate designs that meet national cleanup levels that are based on realistic assumptions and practices concerning risks. If the party liable for cleanup believes it can devise an even cheaper remedy that can meet the national health standards, it can perform a site-specific risk analysis to make its case to EPA. This option allows parties to propose remedies based on the ultimate goal of protecting health and the environment, rather than on the "intermediate" targets of reductions in soil or water concentrations, and helps tailor remedies chosen for a site to its particular features.

Most important, a factor in the remedy selection process at individual sites will be a comparison of the reasonableness of costs against several measures of effectiveness. This approach introduces discipline, transparency, and recognition of tradeoffs into the remedy selection process, while retaining consideration of other factors such as community acceptance and meeting the primary criterion of protecting health and the environment. Cost will also be considered in decisions on whether to defer final cleanups for cases where a new technology is on the horizon to replace a current one that has disproportionately high costs.

The Liability System

The transactions' costs associated with cleanups, especially litigation expenses, have been massive under current law. One study found that these costs account for 19 to 27 percent of all Superfund costs. Transaction costs are substantial in part because liability under current law is strict, joint and several, and retroactive: A party that contributed waste to a site used by others can be held liable for the entire cost of cleanup, and a party is liable for the results of its dumping even if its action was legal at the time. As a result, potentially responsible parties (PRPs) have strong incentives to contest their liability (resulting in high enforcement costs to the EPA), to sue other PRPs to recover costs, and to sue their insurance companies when the latter refuse to pay related claims.

The Administration's proposal seeks to limit these transactions' costs by streamlining the liability allocation process and making it more fair. The new allocation process is based upon nonbinding arbitration, in which PRPs are assigned a share of liability based on factors such as the volume and toxicity of their wastes. PRPs who settle for their assigned shares would surrender their rights to pursue other PRPs for contribution, be protected from suits by other PRPs, and be offered, for a fee, protection from future liability arising from remedy failure or undiscovered harms. As an added incentive to settle, the EPA would pay settling parties for their share of the "orphan shares"—the share of liability attributed to an identified but insolvent party—but nonsettling parties could still be held liable for all or part of the "orphan share."

The Administration proposal also addresses the growing problem of Superfund-related insurance litigation. The problem arises because insurance contracts written before Superfund was enacted did not expressly allocate Superfund liabilities. Subsequently, courts in some States have interpreted those contracts to require insurance companies to assume most Superfund liabilities, but courts in some other States have held the opposite. The scope of insurers' liability in most States is undecided. Building on a proposal originally suggested by the insurance industry, the Administration proposal calls for creation of an Environmental Insurance Resolution Fund financed through fees and assessments on property and casualty insurers. If the PRPs can show sufficient insurance coverage before 1986, the fund would be used to settle their insurance claims for cleanup and restoration costs at pre-1986 NPL sites, as well as some costs at non-NPL sites, at rates determined simultaneously for all of a PRP's sites. The combination of the allocation process and the insurance settlement process should substantially reduce transactions costs and increase fairness.

QUESTIONS FOR ANALYSIS

1. What is the role of externalities in causing environmental pollution?

2. What techniques can the government use to reduce pollution? What are the relative advantages and disadvantages of each of these techniques?

3. According to Mr. Brown, "The internationally accepted system of national economic accounting used to calculate gross national product [or gross domestic product] . . . rightly subtracts the depreciation of plant and equipment from the overall output of goods and services, but it takes no account of the depreciation of natural capital—such as the loss of topsoil from erosion, the destruction of forests by acid rain, or the depletion of the protective ozone layer." Is this true? Explain.

4. In Mr. Brown's view, "Basic economics argues for a switch to solar energy. If the eventual consequence of failing to respond is catastrophe, the answer is obvious." What would be the costs to society of such a transition? What would be the benefits? Would the costs and benefits depend on how quickly the switch was made? Are you in favor of such a switch? Why or why not?

5. Mr. Brown argues that: "By far the most effective instrument to transform the economy quickly . . . is tax policy, specifically, the partial replacement of income taxes with environmental taxes." What sort of environmental taxes does he have in mind? What groups would be hurt most by such taxes? Would you favor the partial replacement of income taxes with environmental taxes? Why or why not?

6. According to President Clinton's Council of Economic Advisers, the fees that the federal government charges ranchers to graze animals on federal land "should reflect both the value of the forage used by an additional animal and the external environmental costs of grazing an additional animal (such as the value of reduction in recreation or water quality)." Why? Aren't federal lands a resource that should be used? Don't ranchers help to pay for federal lands through their tax payments?

7. President Clinton's Council of Economic Advisers criticizes existing government regulations whereby "Federal grazing permits have 'use-it-or-lose-it' provisions, under which decreases in the number of animals grazed may result in the loss of a grazing permit or a reduction in the number of animals that the permitholder may graze in the future." What is wrong with such permits? If the holder of a permit makes little or no use of it, why should he or she continue to have this privilege? Isn't the basic idea to make maximum use of federal lands?

8. President Clinton's Council of Economic Advisers supports a requirement "that firms offer employees the option of taking the cash value of their employer-provided parking benefit as taxable income rather than accepting their free parking space." What is this proposed requirement meant to achieve? Do you think it will work? Why or why not?

9. Is it likely that international cooperation will be required to reduce the emission of greenhouse gases? Why or why not? What problems are likely to be encountered in obtaining such cooperation?

10. From the point of view of society as a whole, shouldn't environmental pollution be eliminated completely? After all, our planet can only tolerate so much in the way of pollutants, and it is common knowledge that air pollution in cities like Los Angeles and water pollution in areas like the Chesapeake Bay are very high. Isn't it obvious that we should put a halt to environmental pollution?

PART SIX

PROMOTING

U.S.

ECONOMIC

GROWTH

There is considerable controversy over the sorts of policies
that the government should carry out to promote economic
growth. Ronald Brown, Secretary of Commerce, summarizes
some of the programs, particularly in support of research
and development, initiated by the Clinton Administration.
Linda Cohen of the University of California, Irvine, and
Roger Noll of Stanford University argue that the U.S. has not
yet found a politically workable and economically attractive
way of encouraging technological progress. President
Clinton's Council of Economic Advisers takes up the central
question: How fast can the U.S. economy grow on a sustainable basis?

Federal Promotion of Economic Growth

RONALD H. BROWN*

et me begin, Mr. Chairman, by commending you for holding this hearing and, even more importantly, for asking exactly the right question: How can our efforts today lay the groundwork for a strong and vibrant economy 20 years hence? Our vision of the year 2015 is of a U.S. economy sustained by growth, creating economic opportunities for all of the American people: a place where dynamic American businesses and a highly skilled U.S. workforce use advanced technologies to produce the goods and services that consumers will demand both here at home and all around the world.

To reach that vision requires that we employ each ingredient of sustainable national economic growth: investment, a skilled workforce, open markets and, of course, innovation. It is private investment that drives competition and growth. It is critical to support private investment through sustained progress on cutting the federal deficit. That is why President Clinton fought so hard—and so successfully—for a deficit reduction that got government out of businesses' way in our capital markets. The result: since the end of 1992, business investment in plant and equipment has increased at an annual rate of 14 percent.

For firms to succeed, it also is necessary that we have an educated, well-

---

*This was testimony before the House Science Committee on January 6, 1995. Ronald Brown is Secretary of Commerce.

trained workforce. To continue to be the most competitive nation in the world, we need the best workforce in the world, and that is why the President's middle class tax cut is focused on education and training.

Opening markets for U.S. businesses has been a priority of this Administration. The passage of the North American Free Trade Agreement (NAFTA) and of the Uruguay Round GATT agreement will create enormous potential for world trade and economic growth. The Administration's "National Export Strategy" is helping U.S. companies—small, medium and large—realize their full potential.

Each of these three ingredients is integrally linked to the fourth, innovation. Indeed, in each of these areas, the Administration has taken action that is focused directly on the importance of innovation—ranging from extension of the R&E tax credit and a targeted capital gains reduction for investments in small business, to boosting educational opportunities for our young people, to freeing $32 billion in exports by reducing unnecessary controls on U.S. computer, telecommunications and electronics products. Through all of these efforts, innovation is being spurred.

The close connection between innovation and economic performance has been reconfirmed by new research from the Commerce Department's Economics Statistics Administration released last month. That report found that firms that use advanced technologies are more productive, pay higher wages, offer more secure jobs and increase employment more rapidly than firms that do not.

Chart 6 illustrates the vital role that industry-government partnership

CHART 6   Enabling the Nation's Capacity to Perform in a Global Community

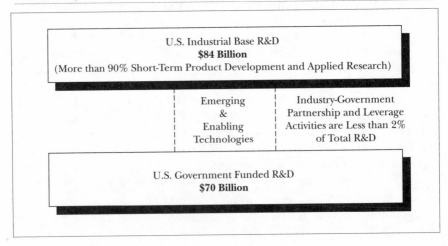

and leveraging activities play in the progress of science and technology. U.S. industry invests more than 90 percent of the $84 billion it spends annually on short-term product development and applied research. In today's fiercely competitive global marketplace, in which product life cycles are measured in months, industry's focus *must* be on short-term product and process innovations.

On the other hand, the U.S. government makes longer term investments in basic science and mission-oriented research and development. That's where the $70 billion spent by our government goes, such as in my own department's National Institute of Standards and Technology laboratories and NOAA basic research.

As Chart 7 shows, 58 percent of the Federal government's R&D funding relates to the mission of defense. A majority of Federal R&D expenditures are devoted to basic and mission-oriented research. As Chart 6 showed, industry-government partnerships and leverage activities are less than 2 percent of government-funded R&D.

Like any portfolio, the mix of R&D activities must reflect a balance between long-term and short-term goals.

While research and applied science are vital components of our innovation portfolio, and while short-term commercialization is necessary and, in

CHART 7   Federal R&D Funding for Defense & Civilian Functions, 1993

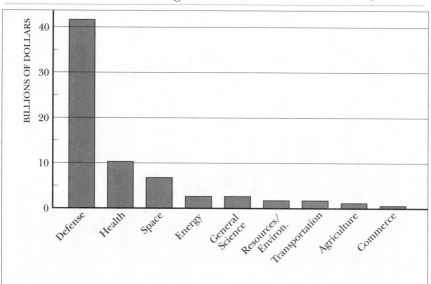

Sources: NSF "Federal R&D Funding by Budget Function: FY 1991–93" and unpublished NSF data.

fact, essential—it is not enough. We have learned over the past 20 years that, all too often, U.S. discoveries of basic knowledge were better exploited by other countries that were better able to develop applicable technologies and transform them into competitive products and services. The marketplace alone will not invest sufficient resources into mid- and longer-term, broad-based technology development needed by the private sector to fully exploit basic knowledge. Our industry-led technology development partnerships are an important link between basic science and private-sector commercialization. These funds promise widespread economic benefits to our nation. This critical fraction of a percent helps build the industrial base we need to support our national and our economic security, and we believe that it must be supported. To do otherwise would be tantamount to unilateral disarmament in the global marketplace.

Consider the major R&D expenditures of our major trading partners, which are illustrated in Chart 8. As a percentage of GDP, we lag behind Japan and Germany, and are roughly on a par with France and the United Kingdom. Our Advanced Technology Program (ATP) helps address the shortfall.

By sharing the costs of research, Commerce's ATP program reduces the risk for private businesses, thus allowing them to conduct R&D that might otherwise not be conducted at all. Through a rigorous, merit-based review, the ATP program ensures that funded research has both technological and commercial potential. And, with a bottom-up, private-sector approach, the

CHART 8   National Nondefense R&D as a Percentage of GDP, by Country, 1981, 1986, 1991

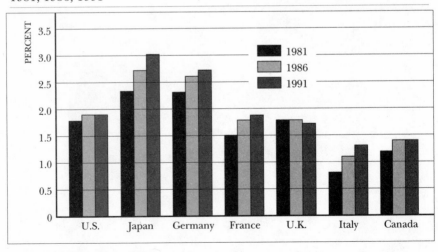

Sources: NSF S&E Indicators 1993.

ATP program maintains private-sector priorities, not government fiat, as the driving force for technological achievement and focus.

The first four years of the ATP have shown small businesses to be eager participants: as Chart 9 shows, of the awards made since 1990, *roughly half have been to individual small businesses or joint ventures led by small businesses.*

Diamond Semiconductor Group of Gloucester, Massachusetts, is a perfect example of this emphasis. This company was a two-person operation with a promising, but unrealized innovation in semiconductor manufacturing. They hoped to develop a new type of ion implantation machine, one of the primary tools of the industry. The new machine would be smaller, faster, cheaper and more accurate than existing devices but it required design breakthroughs considered very difficult. And expensive. The real payoff would come from their ability to produce 12-inch semiconductor wafers rather than 8-inch wafers, like this one.

The concept wasn't easy to sell. Diamond's President spent a year and a half looking for funding, and I know there is this theory out there that venture capitalists will fund anything, but they won't fund anything. They want something that they can feel or touch, and move quickly to commercialization. Diamond's efforts proved unsuccessful and they began considering overseas investors. Fortunately, the partners decided to first apply for an ATP award. Their project was one of 21 selected in 1992.

CHART 9   ATP Awards 1990–1994 By Type of Organization

Awardees include 158 small business, 221 medium/large businesses, and 32 universities. One hundred subcontracts have also gone to universities.

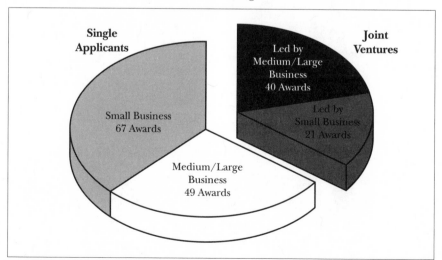

Today, with a contract with one of the country's largest semiconductor equipment manufacturers in hand, Diamond has 35 full- and part-time employees. The partners credit the company's success—and in fact, its very existence—to the ATP award for a high-risk technology that only became attractive to a private-sector investor once it was shown to be feasible.

Stimulating the development of innovative technologies is only half of the equation. The other half—getting new and existing products to market in a timely, cost-effective, competitive basis—is also critical if U.S. firms are to succeed in the global marketplace.

America's 370,000 small and medium-sized manufacturers will have easy access to modern manufacturing technologies, production techniques and best practices through the Manufacturing Extension Partnership (MEP) national system, which is illustrated on Chart 10. These MEP centers are industry-driven, responsive and focused on positive bottom-line impacts.

Mr. Chairman, you can see that we are serious about reaching out to small and medium-sized businesses to help make them more productive and more competitive, and to put new technology—not only high technology, but all technology—into the hands of entrepreneurs, so they can help us create economic growth and jobs. If my testimony today has emphasized anything it is this: We live in an increasingly competitive global economy in which all aspects of economic competitiveness are integrally connected.

CHART 10   NIST Manufacturing Extension Partnership

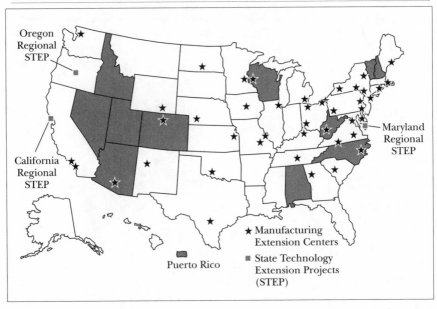

The Department of Commerce is where these connections are made. Some have suggested that we need to create a new "Department of the Future." I respectfully submit, Mr. Chairman, that what we need—what America's businesses, communities and workers need—is a department focused on export growth; focused on technological innovation; focused on sustainable development, economic development and sound economic analysis. The "Department of the Future," in other words, is today's Department of Commerce.

Within our ten bureaus, we work better, in every respect, because we are, every day, confronted with the intersection of trade promotion, civilian technology, economic development, sustainable development and economic analysis.

That intersection is where the future of the United States economy is being fashioned, every day, by entrepreneurs who forge our future one deal, one contract and one transaction at a time. This Administration, my Department of Commerce, and all of us here at the witness table, work with them every day, to our mutual—and our future—benefit.

Thank you.

Privatizing Public Research

Linda R. Cohen

Roger G. Noll

LINDA R. COHEN AND ROGER G. NOLL*

Political support for federally funded research and development is apparently beginning to unravel. Adjusted for inflation, the government's R&D expenditures have fallen 7 percent since 1988. Spending on R&D in the private sector is still increasing, but its growth has fallen below the rate at which output is increasing. Investment in research is not keeping pace with the economy.

In large part, these trends reflect a fundamental change in the rationale for federal research expenditures. From the beginning of World War II through the late 1980s, national security concerns dominated R&D policy. More than half the federal R&D budget was devoted to defense technology, and much of the rest—including fundamental research in mathematics and the physical sciences—received support because of its potential relevance to national security. The end of the cold war weakened this justification for federal research policies.

During the past decade, government officials have sought new goals for their research dollars. The most important emerging theme in their programs is international competitiveness: the federal government should support R&D to increase American industrial productivity, thereby helping industry in global economic competition.

*This is an excerpt from *Scientific American,* September, 1994. Linda Cohen is a professor of economics at the University of California, Irvine, and Roger Noll is a professor in the economics department at Stanford University.

116

We believe the new competitiveness rationale will not succeed in reinvigorating the national R&D effort. First, competitiveness is not a politically powerful substitute for the cold war in forging a durable, bipartisan coalition for supporting R&D at the generous levels typical of past decades. Second, the methods for implementing the new programs are shaped by political necessity and so are likely to undermine the economic performance of the programs. Eventually, that will further reduce the political support for the programs.

Historically, the desire to help an industry increase productivity has always played some role in R&D policy. Federal subsidies for commercially relevant R&D are more than 100 years old, having supported the development of the telegraph and hybrid seeds in the 19th century. Nevertheless, commercial programs did not become a significant component of federal R&D support until World War II. Even then, these programs were almost exclusively targeted at defense-related technologies.

Not until the 1960s did the federal government undertake a broad array of research programs for primarily civilian purposes. These programs were not part of a coherent plan for fostering national economic growth. Instead they were a series of largely unrelated responses to much narrower public issues that gave rise to new "missions" for federal agencies. Examples were the war on cancer, the drive to develop environmentally benign technologies and attempts to find an effective response to the rise of the worldwide oil cartel.

Despite these initiatives, most federal R&D dollars were still spent on defense or on fundamental knowledge directly relevant to defense. Most proposals to broaden the base of these programs—either by adopting a comprehensive commercial R&D policy or by adding more industries to the list of those receiving support—were defeated. In contrast, the current approach to R&D is essentially economy-wide. Its appeal rests on the argument that it can help U.S. industry boost productivity and reclaim dominance in international markets. Almost any industry is a possible target for support.

The competitiveness theme has caused two major changes in how federal R&D programs are formulated and managed. One change is greater privatization of the selection and results of research projects. Privatization is perhaps most clearly evident in the extent to which the new programs assign to private industry both responsibility for decisions about technical choices in the projects and essentially all the intellectual property rights. The other change is increased collaboration among American firms and research organizations.

The most extreme example of these changes is in the open competitions held by the National Institutes of Standards and Technology for its Advanced Technology Program (ATP). Any firm or group of firms, in any industry, can submit a proposal for partial federal funding for a technology development project. Proposals are evaluated by criteria that include potential commercial success, a feasible commercialization and marketing strategy, technical interest, inability to obtain complete private backing for the project and the likelihood of broad applications. These projects need not relate to any specific government mission. Indeed, the program avoids projects intended to provide technology for use by a government agency such as the Department of Defense.

Most of the funds for carrying out the new competitiveness strategy still go to programs that superficially retain more of a public-sector focus. The Technology Reinvestment Program, administered by the Advanced Research Projects Agency in the Department of Defense, has an annual budget of more than half a billion dollars. Its goal is to support projects that will allow firms to rely on commercial markets and profits while developing technologies useful for defense. In addition, several large industry-specific programs have been established, including Sematech (for semi-conductor manufacturing technology), the flat-panel display program, the Clean Coal Technology Program, the National Aerospace Plane Consortium and the Clean Car Initiative. All of them receive substantial federal monies.

To help justify their own continued existence, the federally funded national laboratories are also seeking to conduct joint research with companies. These efforts are called Cooperative Research and Development Agreements (CRADAs). Like the ATP projects, CRADAs are available for all industries and need no connection to any government program.

Despite their contributions from the public sector, these undertakings all diverge from traditional Department of Defense and Department of Energy R&D programs. Commercial technology development is a primary goal rather than an unsought (but welcome) spin-off from carrying out a government mission. Each venture relies on the private participants to propose and manage the projects. Each requires that property rights belong to the private participants rather than to the government sponsor or partner. All the activities require private enterprises to share in the costs. As with the ATP, these programs involve an unusual amount of proprietary information. Project proposals, for example, are routinely exempted from the Freedom of Information Act and are reviewed exclusively by government agencies.

The principle that economic growth is enhanced by new technology has a firm foundation in theoretical and empirical research in economics and has been investigated by several distinguished economists, among them Nobel laureate Robert M. Solow of the Massachusetts Institute of Technology, the late Edward Denison of the Brookings Institution, Moses Abramovitz of Stanford University, Edwin Mansfield of the University of Pennsylvania, Richard Nelson of Columbia University and Zvi Griliches and

Fredric M. Scherer of Harvard University. The main conclusions from their work are that more than half the historical growth in per capita income in the U.S. is attributable to advances in technology and that the total economic return on investment in R&D is several times as high as that for other forms of investment.

That R&D can enhance the nation's economic welfare is not, by itself, sufficient reason to justify a prominent role for the federal government in financing it. Economists have developed a further rationale for government subsidies. Their consensus is that most of the benefits of innovation accrue not to innovators but to consumers through products that are better or less expensive, or both. Because the benefits of technological progress are broadly shared, innovators lack the financial incentive to improve technologies as much as is socially desirable. Therefore, the government can improve the performance of the economy by adopting policies that facilitate and increase investments in research.

In principle, government can solve the problem of underinvestment in R&D in two ways. The first, which political conservatives tend to emphasize, is to promote the ability of innovators to obtain higher profits. In the past, the most important policy for augmenting the profitability of innovation has been to strengthen intellectual property rights: patents, copyrights and legal protection of trade secrets.

This approach has two significant drawbacks. First, it creates higher profits through the establishment of monopolies, which are inefficient. Second, any form of protection for intellectual property limits the diffusion of the research results. Research often has applications in a variety of products and industries; the possible benefits of a discovery can be realized only if people other than the discoverers have the opportunity and incentive to apply those findings in new ways.

The other approach, which liberals tend to favor, is for the government to pay for R&D through targeted programs. In this case, the government selects specific technologies and projects; it then either subsidizes them in the private sector or undertakes them in government research laboratories. This approach, too, has drawbacks. If the goal of the program is to encourage commercial successes, the government is not likely to pick the best projects. Furthermore, monitoring public research projects to assure that private contractors are putting forth their best efforts is notoriously difficult.

The root of the monitoring problem is uncertainty about both the costs and the results of R&D projects. By the very nature of R&D, costs and results are imperfectly known—otherwise the research would not have to be done in the first place. Consequently, the government faces difficulties in specifying realistic technical approaches and objectives. Moreover, early work on a project is likely to generate information that moves the government to change the details of the project. Contracts are therefore often based on a cost-reimbursement formula. Unfortunately, such contracts are well known for their tendency to produce cost overruns.

The government's traditional safeguard against companies that take advantage of cost and performance uncertainties is to impose rigorous cost-accounting and auditing requirements on R&D contractors in a herculean effort to find waste, fraud and lax management. This monitoring system applies to most of the new programs, and it is far more elaborate, costly and inflexible than the monitoring systems that private organizations employ for their own research. As a result, R&D done under federal contract is inherently more expensive and less effective than R&D done by an organization using its own funds. In fact, government monitoring methods are so burdensome that many federal contractors separate their federal and private work so that they can use more flexible, cheaper methods for managing their private R&D. . . .

Our conclusion is that the U.S. has not yet found a politically workable and economically attractive means of encouraging technological progress. Both economic research on R&D and the historical experience with government programs indicate that the most effective solution would be a combination of policies. The government would take a directing role in subsidizing both fundamental research and research aimed at broadening the technology base. It would make the results of that research widely available rather than proprietary. For applications research, the government can probably encourage development and avoid political pitfalls only if it follows a completely hands-off policy (say, by providing differential tax treatment for research investment) or if it concentrates on small schemes in carefully selected industries. The latter strategy is unlikely to have any wide-ranging impact on economic performance.

Unfortunately, this approach entails significant political liabilities. Consumers would benefit the most—but most of the political support for R&D comes from industry, not consumers. And because the entities that conduct technology-base research cannot usually keep the results for themselves, U.S. firms would not be the only beneficiaries. In the current political lexicon, a "competitiveness" strategy is one with policies that focus on short-term commercial products and exclude foreign companies from sharing in the benefits. That interpretation is fundamentally at odds with the broader concept of promoting innovation.

The breadth and intensity of the federal R&D programs that this nation has enjoyed in the past have richly contributed to the growth of its economy. Maintaining that support, however, hinges on building a strong, stable consensus for it. Competitiveness cannot replace national security as the basis for that consensus.

How Fast Can the U.S. Economy Grow?

PRESIDENT CLINTON'S COUNCIL OF ECONOMIC ADVISERS*

How fast can the economy grow on a sustainable basis? Most mainstream analysts currently believe that aggregate output can grow about 2.5 percent per year. Recently, however, some analysts—perhaps inspired by the outstanding performance of the economy in 1994—have asserted that much more rapid growth, possibly as fast as 5 percent per year, may be sustainable.

The answer to this question has profound implications for the future well-being of the American people. If the mainstream view is correct, aggregate output will double only every 28 years or so, and per capita output only about every 56 years (assuming population growth of 1 percent per year). But if the alternative view is correct, aggregate output could double every 14 years, and per capita output every 18 years.

The answer also has important implications for the conduct of government policy. Sensible Federal budget planning can proceed only in the context of a realistic assessment of the long-term outlook for the economy. If the outlook is robust, then a more expansionary fiscal policy may well be consistent with a responsible outcome on the deficit. If, on the other hand, the outlook is more subdued, a greater degree of fiscal restraint may be required.

*This is an excerpt from the *Economic Report of the President* (Washington, D.C.: Government Printing Office, 1995).

Chart 11 illustrates one simple method for assessing the sustainable rate of growth of gross domestic product (GDP). . . . The chart focuses on the growth of real GDP between the first quarter of 1988 and the fourth quarter of 1994. The reason for focusing on these two quarters is that the unemployment rate was very similar in both: 5.7 percent and 5.6 percent, respectively. This suggests that a similar fraction of the economy's overall productive capacity was being utilized in both quarters. Thus the average rate of growth of output in the interval between them should give a good indication of the average rate of growth of the economy's productive capacity during that period.

As the chart shows, real GDP increased at an average annual rate of 2.1 percent between the first quarter of 1988 and the fourth quarter of 1994. This suggests that the economy's productive capacity—potential GDP—also grew at about that rate. Over the same period, real GDP measured on the more conventional basis (1987 dollars) increased at an average annual rate of 2.3 percent. Therefore, this simple method suggests that the con-

CHART 11   Real Gross Domestic Product

Between the beginning of 1988 and the end of 1994, real GDP increased at an average annual rate of 2.1 percent.

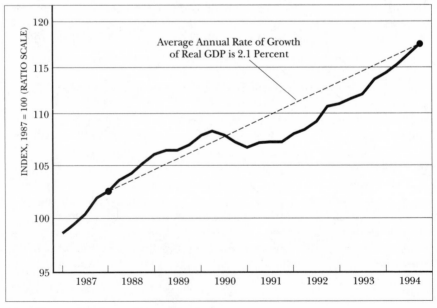

Note: Data are based on a chain-weighted measure.

Source: Department of Commerce.

sensus view that the sustainable rate of growth is about 2 1/2 percent per year is slightly more optimistic than a purely mechanical reading of recent experience would warrant. . . .

FACTORS GENERATING GROWTH OF POTENTIAL GDP

Between 1963 and 1994 real U.S. GDP increased at an average annual rate of 3.1 percent per year. Because the economy appears to have been operating about at its potential in both those years, the average rate of growth of *actual* output between those dates should provide a relatively accurate estimate of the average rate of growth of *potential* output during the same period.

Growth of real GDP can be decomposed into two main components: growth of output per hour worked (or productivity) and growth of hours worked. As Chart 12 illustrates, these two components each contributed 1.7 percentage points to the growth of GDP between 1963 and 1994. (Strictly speaking, the data on productivity and hours worked pertain only to the private nonfarm business sector, whereas the data on output pertain to the

CHART 12   Factors Generating Growth of Gross Domestic Product

Since 1972, real GDP has increased more slowly than before, owing to a reduction in the rate of growth of output per hour worked.

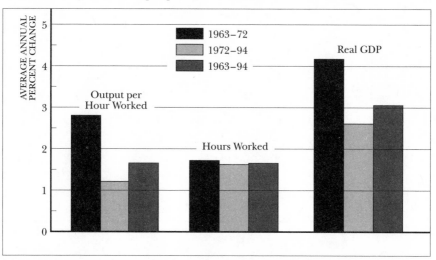

Note: Estimates of growth in output and output per hour are based on chain-weighted measures. Data on output per hour and hours worked pertain to the private nonfarm business sector, whereas the data on GDP pertain to the whole economy.

Sources: Council of Economic Advisers, Department of Commerce, and Department of Labor.

total economy. As a result, and because the output of the private nonfarm business sector was increasing slightly more rapidly than the output of the total economy, the growth of output per hour and the growth of hours worked add up to slightly more than the growth of GDP).

Chart 12 also shows that the average experience since 1963 subsumes two very different episodes. Between 1963 and 1972 real GDP increased at an average annual rate of 4.2 percent. By contrast, since 1972 real GDP has increased only about 2.6 percent per year. (The economy appears to have been operating at about its potential in 1972; as a result, that year should also serve as a useful benchmark for purposes of estimating potential GDP growth rates.) The slower rate of growth of GDP since 1972 can be attributed to a slowdown in the rate of growth of productivity, since the growth of hours worked was about as rapid after 1972 as before.

Chart 13 examines the slowdown in the growth of productivity in more detail. The chart illustrates one of the most significant economic developments of the postwar period. Whereas productivity in the private nonfarm

CHART 13 Output per Hour in the Private Nonfarm Business Sector

Productivity growth in the private nonfarm business sector seems to have slowed markedly sometime in the early 1970s.

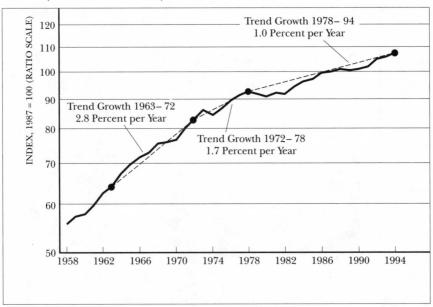

Note: Data are based on a chain-weighted measure.

Sources: Council of Economic Advisers and Department of Labor.

business sector increased at an average annual rate of 2.8 percent between 1963 and 1972, it increased only 1.7 percent per year between 1972 and 1978, and only 1.0 percent after 1978 (yet another year in which the economy was operating close to potential).

By contrast, productivity growth in the manufacturing sector seems to have slowed much less during the past four decades. As Chart 14 shows, output per hour in the manufacturing sector is estimated to have increased on average about 3.3 percent per year between 1963 and 1972, 2.6 percent between 1972 and 1978, and 2.6 percent again between 1978 and 1987. . . .

Taken together, Charts 13 and 14 suggest that the slowdown in the growth of productivity after 1972 was concentrated outside the manufacturing sector. It has been argued that these and similar data exaggerate that concentration, because they do not control for the fact that the manufacturing sector may have increasingly "outsourced" some low-productivity activities. For example, if factories contract with security firms to do work formerly done by their own security guards, that activity will be counted in the services rather than the manufacturing sector, and if security guards'

CHART 14 Output per Hour in the Manufacturing Sector

Productivity growth in the manufacturing sector appears to have slowed only a little since the 1960s and early 1970s.

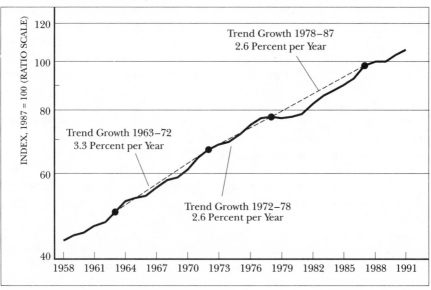

Note: Data are based on a chain-weighted measure.

Source: Department of Labor.

productivity is less than that of the factories' assembly-line workers, official statistics may report an increase in overall manufacturing productivity that does not reflect an increase in the productivity of any individual worker. What this argument ignores, however, is that *high*-productivity jobs may also have been outsourced, in which case the direction of bias in the official estimates would be ambiguous. On balance, the evidence suggests that the apparent strength of productivity growth in manufacturing is not a figment of job migration.

Much of the discussion in this chapter focuses on the slow rate of growth of productivity in the United States since the early 1970s, relative to earlier U.S. experience and the experience of other countries. But it is worth noting that U.S. workers remain among the most productive in the world. This suggests that the productivity "problem" in the United States has much more to do with the rate of growth of productivity than with its level. . . .

HAS THE TREND IN PRODUCTIVITY GROWTH IMPROVED RECENTLY?

Since 1987, according to current estimates, productivity growth in the private nonfarm business sector has averaged 1.2 percent per year, somewhat faster than the average during the previous decade. And since 1991, productivity growth has averaged about 2.0 percent per year—more than twice the 1978–87 average. Are recent claims of a pickup in trend productivity growth justified? (Provided there has been no offsetting reduction in the growth of hours, such a pickup would translate into an increase in the economy's potential growth rate.) This question is not easily resolved because the recent behavior of productivity has been heavily influenced (for the better) by the faster pace of economic activity during the last 2 years. A proper assessment of the trend in productivity growth can be made only by abstracting from cyclical influences.

Chart 15 focuses on the behavior of productivity since 1976. Between 1978 and 1982—a period that included the deepest recession of the postwar period—productivity actually declined slightly according to official estimates. Then, as recovery took hold, productivity rebounded. By 1987 the economy once again was operating in the neighborhood of its full potential. Between 1978 and 1987 the growth of productivity averaged about 0.9 percent per year.

Since 1987 this chain of events has essentially repeated itself: a period of slow growth in productivity as the economy endured a recession, followed by a period of rebound as the recovery gathered strength. Today, well into the expansion, the economy once again appears to be operating in the neighborhood of its potential. Between 1987 and 1994—as was noted above—productivity growth averaged about 1.2 percent per year. Thus,

CHART 15 Output per Hour in the Private Nonfarm Business Sector

Productivity has increased rapidly since 1991. Nonetheless, it is still difficult to know whether there has been an improvement in the trend rate of productivity growth.

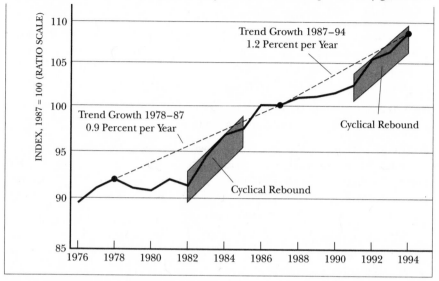

Note: Data are based on a chain-weighted measure.

Sources: Council of Economic Advisers and Department of Labor.

currently available data do seem to hint that the trend in productivity growth has picked up in the last few years. However, the magnitude of that pickup pales in comparison to the decline that occurred earlier in the postwar period. Moreover, the evidence in support of a pickup is still inconclusive. For example, if trends are computed for the periods 1978–86 and 1986–94 rather than 1978–87 and 1987–94, the suggestion of a pickup is much weaker: productivity growth averaged 1.0 percent per year in the earlier alternative subperiod and 1.1 percent in the later one. On the other hand, if the breakpoint chosen is 1988 or, especially, 1989, the evidence in favor of a pickup appears stronger. However, the averages over these later periods, especially the one since 1989, are dominated by the cyclical recovery and so may create a false impression of an improvement in the trend.

Furthermore, the Labor Department released data in 1994 suggesting that the growth of hours worked between 1993 and 1994 may be revised upward by enough to shave 0.1 percentage point off the average rate of productivity increase for the period 1987–94. Thus, while the evidence in favor of a slight improvement in the productivity growth trend is encouraging, it is not yet decisive. The experience of the next few years will be quite telling for this issue.

QUESTIONS FOR ANALYSIS

1. Secretary Brown's testimony was directed to the question: "How can our efforts today lay the groundwork for a strong and vibrant economy 20 years hence?" How does he answer this question?

2. According to Mr. Brown, "The marketplace alone will not invest sufficient resources into mid- and longer-term, broad-based technology development needed by the private sector to fully exploit basic knowledge." Why not? Does the paper by Professors Cohen and Noll help to answer this question?

3. Secretary Brown describes the Commerce Department's Advanced Technology Program (ATP). What are its major features?

4. Professors Cohen and Noll argue that, with the end of the cold war, national defense has been replaced by international competitiveness as the rationale for federal funding of research. In their view, "Competitiveness cannot replace national security as the basis for that consensus." Why not? Do you agree? Why or why not?

5. Professors Cohen and Noll point out that in principle, "government can solve the problem of underinvestment in R&D in two ways." What are they? What are the advantages and disadvantages of each one?

6. Why do Cohen and Noll believe that a "competitiveness" strategy is "fundamentally at odds with the broader concept of promoting innovation"? Do you agree? Why or why not?

7. President Clinton's Council of Economic Advisers is concerned with the question: How fast can the economy grow on a sustainable basis? Why is this question of fundamental importance?

8. The Council suggests that "the productivity 'problem' in the United States has much more to do with the rate of growth of productivity than with its level." What do they mean?

9. Does the available evidence indicate that the trend in productivity growth has improved since the late 1980s?

10. Would you favor public policies designed to increase the rate of productivity growth in the United States? Why or why not?

PART SEVEN

FISCAL POLICY

Everyone who reads a newspaper or watches television must be aware that the United States is running a very large budget deficit. In the first article, Peter Peterson, chairman of the Blackstone Group and former secretary of commerce, argues that entitlements programs like Social Security and Medicare must be cut back, and that the middle class must be prepared for sacrifices. The second article shows how two major publications—*Business Week* and the *Philadelphia Inquirer*—would cut government spending. The third article is a debate between Robert Hall and Alvin Rabushka of Stanford University, who favor a flat tax, and Robert Kuttner of the *American Prospect,* who opposes it.

The Third Rail of American Politics

PETER PETERSON*

I can't remember who it was who first said that you could take all the economists in the world, lay them end to end—and still not reach a conclusion. But if you listen carefully to most economists and policy experts today, there is actually a great deal of consensus about the magnitude of America's economic challenges and what sorts of reforms will be necessary to overcome them.

In particular, most would agree to the following: (1) To get American living standards rising again, we must increase productivity. (2) To boost productivity we must invest more—much, much more—not just in machines, but in R&D, in infrastructure, and in people. Many, myself included, think that *at least $400 billion a year in new investments are needed.* (3) This in turn means we must save much, much more—*$400 billion a year more.* (4) The surest and fastest way to increase our savings is to reduce and eventually eliminate the federal deficit, which is really just a form of "negative" public savings. (5) To reduce the deficit and keep it down we must make major cuts in consumption spending, and in particular in entitlements. But this, alas, requires us to confront a brute question: If we are to save more by consuming less, *whose* consumption growth do we propose to cut?

It's at this point that agreement on what needs to be done—while not ex-

*This is an excerpt from Peter Peterson, *Facing Up* (New York: Simon and Schuster, 1994). Peter Peterson is chairman of the Blackstone Group and a former secretary of commerce.

actly breaking down—comes face-to-face with a truth that remains politically inexpressible. That truth is that the problem is all of us. *Most Americans—emphatically including the middle class—will have to give something up, at least temporarily, to get back our American Dream.*

We all remember Bill Clinton's damning campaign slogan: "It's the economy, stupid." Well, when it comes to the budget the watchword ought to be "It's entitlements, stupid." From Social Security and Medicare to farm aid and federal pensions, it is these benefit programs that dominate the budget today. In 1993, entitlement outlays totaled a staggering $761 billion—or 54 percent of all federal spending. And that doesn't include $150 billion more in back-door benefits passed out through the tax code, such as the deduction for home mortgage interest and the exclusion from taxable income of employer-paid health care. (These subsidies, which are the fiscal equivalent of a check in the mail, are technically called "tax expenditures.")

CHART 16   Federal Spending by Major Budget Functions and Federal Deficit

Entitlement spending dominates the federal budget.

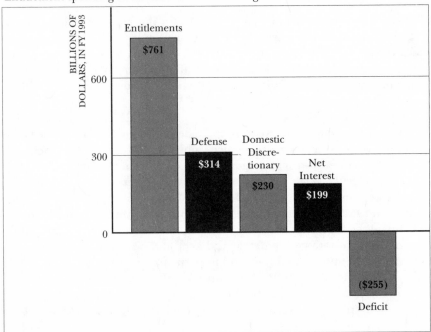

Note: Budget functions are defined by the Congressional Budget Office. Defense includes "International" discretionary spending.

It is the explosive growth in entitlements, moreover, that threatens to rob our future. I've already noted that even with the Clinton deficit reduction package in place, entitlement outlays are slated to grow by $393 billion in today's dollars between 1994 and 2004. This means that, along with interest costs, they will account for all growth in federal spending over the next decade. In fact, apart from entitlements and net interest, other federal outlays are actually scheduled to decline by $31 billion in real terms between 1994 and 2004. If this seems surprising, recall that the President is aggressively clipping the Pentagon's wings—so that by 1998 we will be spending less on defense, as a share of GDP, than in any year since Pearl Harbor. As for future domestic discretionary spending—for everything from R&D and space exploration to immigration control and law enforcement—this too is expected to shrink as a share of GDP, and by 1997 will have sunk back beneath the postwar record low it reached late in the Reagan administration.

The usual solutions no longer apply. Even if we immediately and permanently cut defense spending by half, twenty years from now we would again

CHART 17 Projected Changes in Federal Spending from FY 1994 to FY 2004 by Major Budget Function

Along with interest payments, entitlements will account for all real federal spending growth over the next decade.

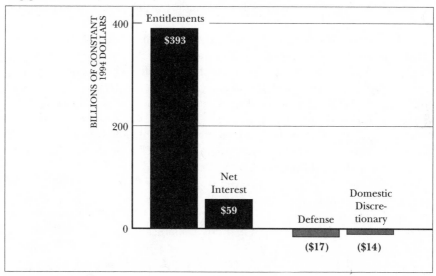

Note: Budget projections by the Congressional Budget Office. Defense includes "International" discretionary spending.

face the same deficit burden as today. We can keep raising tax rates, but to keep up with the growth of entitlements alone we would have to enact a new tax hike, equal to the one sponsored by President Clinton, roughly every four years for the next half century. What we must now confront is the need to cut entitlements.

President Clinton, it's true, never promised to leave all entitlements untouched. But he did make a sweeping social promise that was just as unfortunate in its effects. He assured the public that nothing in his budget would take much away from any household belonging to the "middle class." According to Clinton's definition, moreover, only about 1 percent of all U.S. tax filers—for example, joint-filing couples with gross incomes over $200,000—are too rich to be included in the middle class.

As a guide to tax reform, Clinton's promise was unfortunate enough. Americans with incomes over $200,000 earn just 13 percent of all pretax income in the United States. It shouldn't take any arcane knowledge of fiscal arithmetic to see that balancing the budget on such a narrow stretch of income territory is quite literally impossible. In fact, if President Clinton had wanted to balance the budget by taxing the "rich" alone, he would have had to tax away *all* the taxable income of everyone with more than $175,000 of gross income. Or, taking a less draconian approach, he might merely have *doubled* the income taxes of the "affluent"—but that would have required including everyone down to about $50,000 of income. Even this kinder and gentler approach would amount to something like expropriation—hardly the kind of policy consistent with either free markets or democracy.

But Clinton's promise to the middle class was most damaging in its impact on entitlement reform, since it precluded major savings from the largest and fastest growing part of the budget. Households with incomes over $200,000 received just 1 percent ($5 billion) of federal entitlement outlays in 1991. No one is—or should be—talking about significant entitlement cuts for lower-income Americans. That leaves all households with incomes above the U.S. household median—roughly $30,000 in 1991—yet below $200,000, in other words, that part of Clinton's "middle class," which, however hard-pressed, cannot claim to be destitute.

In 1991, such households received no less than 43 percent of all benefit dollars ($227 billion) disbursed under major Federal entitlement programs. It is worth noting, moreover, that this absolute dollar figure almost certainly understates the total benefit dollars going to the $30,000 to $200,000 income bracket, since it only reflects the 80 percent of entitlement outlays flowing through programs for which we have accurate income data on recipients. What about the remaining 20 percent? We cannot be sure. Some of it flows through programs such as Medicaid, which mostly benefit lower-income households; some too flows through programs such as student loans, farm aid, and veterans' health care, which disproportionately benefit upper-income households. All told, it would be safe to assume that total federal benefit outlays reaching the $30,000 to $200,000 income bracket amounted to at least $265 billion in 1991.

Then consider our ocean of so-called tax expenditures—the subtle subsidies that help Americans borrow huge sums for home mortgages and that underwrite gold-plated employer health plans. Here the share received by Clinton's "middle-class" is larger still. Over two-thirds go to tax filers with incomes between $30,000 and $200,000. Just 7 percent go to the Americans whom the President calls "rich."

The lesson in these numbers seems clear. Any plan to balance the budget that exempts the broad middle class from sacrifice is doomed to failure. But if we are willing to ask for even modest sacrifices from all Americans with incomes above about $30,000, the picture changes entirely. Suddenly we're talking about a whopping 73 percent of national household income. We're also talking about a stunning 74 percent of all tax expenditures and 43 percent of federal entitlement outlays. Taken together, these benefits amounted to $372 billion in 1991. That's a sum that we simply cannot ignore if we are at all serious about putting our fiscal house in order.

Let's pause for a moment to ask ourselves: What in reality is the "middle class"? Ask any American if he or she is "middle class," and the answer will almost always be "yes!" The truly poor will admit to being "lower middle class" and the rich will go along with "upper middle class," but few will forthrightly call themselves "poor" or "rich." This is a characteristically American self-perception, and it reflects our desire to live in a basically egalitarian society. Next, ask any group of Americans to specify the annual income that defines "middle class" and you'll hear responses ranging from, say, $20,000 all the way up to $200,000—if we include the Clinton administration's definition.

But there are more precise and realistic definitions. The median U.S. household income in 1993 (including nontaxable government and employer benefits) was $31,700. If you narrowly define middle class to comprise one-half of all American households, equally distributed around that $31,700 household, the statistical middle-class income turns out to range from $14,040 to $55,880.

This exposition regularly startles those who are new to it. A household with $60,000 of income invariably thinks of itself as "just getting by," but it actually stands in the top quarter of U.S. households. A two-earner couple with an income totaling $120,000 may think of itself as just middle class. In fact, that two-earner couple stands in the top 5 percent of American households. By the time we reach those with incomes in excess of $200,000, we are left with a mere statistical sliver of the population: roughly 1 percent.

Middle-class Americans today, it seems, suffer from what might be called a "reverse Lake Wobegon" syndrome. As Garrison Keillor fans know, Lake Wobegon is a wonderful fictional place where all the children are *above* average. When it comes to incomes, however, most middle-class Americans, trying hard to make ends meet, assume they must be *below* average.

The broad middle class likes to think that because they aren't genuinely rich, they can't possibly be part of the solution to America's economic problems, and that because they aren't truly poor (aren't a dysfunctional family on welfare, for example), they can't possibly be part of the problem itself. Both lines of reasoning are fallacious. As the accompanying charts show, a huge share of the escalating budget for federal benefit programs is not spent on welfare for the poor, as is commonly thought, but on subsidizing the broad middle class. The truth is that middle-income Americans, just like all other Americans, are on the dole—the entitlement dole. But few realize it. Facing up means facing the fact that we are *all* on welfare of one kind or another.

When middle-class benefits come in the form of Social Security and Medicare payments, or military and civil service pensions, they don't seem like *subsidies* in the sense that welfare checks to the poor are. "I've worked hard all my life; I'm just getting what I am entitled to," middle-class retirees say. And there's exactly the problem! . . . [A]*ll of us* have decided that we are *entitled* to much more than our society can afford to pay for—especially if we want to find the means to invest in our children and our collective future.

How to Slash
the Deficit:
Alternative Views

BUSINESS WEEK

How to Cut a Cool
$1 Trillion*

Everybody has a list. The libertarian Cato Institute. The centrist Democratic Progressive Policy Institute. The conservative Heritage
Foundation. The bipartisan Entitlement Commission. And soon
John R. Kasich (R-Ohio), House Budget Committee chairman, will have a
list. At a time when people are being driven stark mad by their April 17 tax
preparations, let's muse about cutting government spending.

Here is *Business Week*'s list of things to cut—and not to cut—to balance
the budget. The goal is a high-growth, low-inflation economy supported by
a simplified tax code. That means not messing around with the tax code in
the name of child or corporate welfare. Yes, we would love a flat tax.

But until we get there, get the ax. The goal is to cut $1 trillion over five
years, give or take a few billion. First, our bias. We freely admit we think it's
O.K. to subsidize U.S. exports as long as foreigners subsidize theirs. But not
a minute longer. We also believe that government spending—in moderation—on basic research and new technology can pay off big. Remember
who built the Internet.

So with that, here's the easy part—change the statistics. Even before Alan
Greenspan suggested it, *Business Week* said the consumer price index over-
stated inflation. Rejiggering the CPI to cut inflation by one percentage
point would save $150 billion in cost-of-living adjustments over five years.

*This editorial appeared in *Business Week* on March 27, 1995.

This is a no-brainer. Shifting people in Medicare and Medicaid from fee-for-service to HMOs would save $400 billion over five years. At $550 billion, we're halfway there.

The rest are finer slices of the salami. The government can save about $40 billion over five years by fee-basing the Federal Aviation Administration; $40 billion in reducing agricultural subsidies; $10 billion in selling the Rural Electrification Administration and federal power administrations; $40 billion by privatizing veterans' medical care and reducing transfer payments to federal retirees; $50 billion by cutting defense spending on big-ticket items; $10 billion in cutting welfare; $5 billion in selling the Tennessee Valley Authority and ending the Small Business Administration; $1.5 billion by dumping strategic petroleum and helium reserves; $1.5 billion by ending below-market timber, grazing, and mineral sales; $30 billion by shrinking the bureaucracy; $50 billion by selling federal property; $10 billion by killing the Farmers Home Administration; $20 billion by cutting retraining programs; $10 billion in Housing & Urban Development spending cuts; $30 billion from selling part of the government's loan portfolio; $15 billion by reducing mass-transit subsidies.

That comes to a tidy sum of $913 billion. Savings on lower government debt service plus higher government revenues, thanks to greater economic growth, easily push *Business Week*'s list over the top. Oh yes, one other thing. It doesn't make much sense to try to cut the budget deficit and reduce taxes at the same time. The average family will gain much more from the lower interest rates that come from deficit reduction than it will from a $10-a-week giveback from the federal government.

How to Slash the Deficit: Alternative Views

THE *PHILADELPHIA INQUIRER*

A Better Balance*

ive trillion dollars. That's what the national debt will reach this year. It means $19,000 in IOUs for every man, woman and child in America. For young people, this reckless borrowing is especially unfair because they will live the longest with its consequences.

Last month, President Clinton proposed a five-year plan for piling another $1 trillion on top of this debt. He calls his plan for continued deficit spending "controlling" the problem. We call it irresponsible. It burdens the economy; it cheats children.

For their part, Republicans in the House say they want spending cuts, but so far they have zeroed in on the poor and disadvantaged.

Clearly, the federal government must do better at reducing waste and fraud in safety-net programs such as food stamps and the working-poor tax credit. But a farsighted Congress would re-invest such savings into job-oriented welfare reform.

The spending-cut plan that the House Budget Committee passed last week avoids specifics, treads lightly on entitlements, and most of its savings would go toward cutting taxes—not the deficit.

The best way to put the U.S. economy on a sound footing is to stop massive borrowing that drains hundreds of billions in savings out of the private sector. Yet the Clinton budget for next year has the deficit at $196.7 billion and rising.

*This editorial appeared in the *Philadelphia Inquirer* on March 19, 1995.

139

Instead, the deficit ought to be *$50 billion–$60 billion lower* than he proposed. If that pace of deficit reduction were continued for four years, the budget would be balanced in 1999.

Here is a plan to slash the deficit in fiscal 1996, which starts in October. This *understates* what can be done because it doesn't include anything worth less than $1 billion. And it spreads the sacrifice broadly and fairly: $24 billion in entitlement cuts, $13 billion in other spending cuts and $17 billion in new tax revenues.

The federal government must stop sending benefits to people who don't really need them. The nonpartisan Concord Coalition has a fair method that doesn't touch the majority of Americans. Taxpayers would add their income, plus the value of their entitlements, such as Social Security, Medicare, certain veterans' compensation and farm payments. If that sum was more than $40,000, their benefits would be reduced based on how far above the $40,000 line the person fell.

The reduction in benefits would be 10 percent in the $40,000–$50,000 range, and 70 percent at $100,000–$110,000. This wouldn't happen overnight, but would be phased in over five years. For Medicare beneficiaries, the means-test would be applied only to the "insurance value"—the value of a person's coverage beyond what he or she pays in premiums—and has nothing to do with how much medical care someone receives.

Saves $10 billion.

The Clinton plan lets the Medicare and Medicaid budgets rise by nearly $28 billion next year. A task force headed by Senator Judd Gregg (R.-N.H.) has recommended slowing the annual increase in Medicare to 7.5 percent by accelerating the use of HMOs, and Medicaid to 4 percent by giving states more flexibility in this federal-state program. While the 4 percent goal may be unrealistic, it is clear that well-run HMOs and other forms of "managed care" can deliver quality care and major savings.

This is the principal alternative to making beneficiaries pay more for their coverage—now that Congress has rejected the responsible course of *comprehensive* health-care reform. By accelerating managed care, the feds ought to reduce the annual increase in Medicare and Medicaid by at least 2 percent.

Saves $5 billion.

The government's cost-of-living formula over-adjusts entitlements, tax brackets and exemptions for inflation, according to experts. It should be made more accurate, using the Congressional Budget Office's conservative estimate that it's about 0.5 percent too high.

Saves $3 billion.

With people living much longer, raise the age for full benefits under Social Security—currently 65—by 3 months every year.

Saves $2 billion.

Federal pensions are generous. Yet last week, a House panel balked at making federal employees pay more toward their retirement benefits. Reasonable, yet politically sensitive, reforms could include stopping inflation-adjustments for nondisabled retirees younger than 62 and reducing the matching money on 401(k) plans.

Saves $2 billion.

As House Majority Leader Dick Armey said when he was a powerless member of the minority, U.S. agriculture subsidies are contradictory to the free market. They should be phased out over several years.

Saves $2 billion.

The Pentagon hasn't scaled back its operations to reflect who won the cold war. The Clinton budget cuts defense substantially, but it ought to be cut by billions more. Examples: Cancel the B-2 Stealth bomber, built to penetrate an Evil Empire whose remnant now can't even knock over Chechnya. Sink the Seawolf submarine. Kill the Milstar satellite system for wartime communications. Cancel the F-22 fighter.

Saves $6 billion.

Scale back intelligence-gathering.

Saves $3 billion.

The space station is super-duper, but not worth the red ink.

Saves $2 billion.

Most small-business successes have nothing to do with the Small Business Administration. Cancel most of its functions—shift anything worthwhile to Commerce.

Saves $1 billion.

Start charging market prices for hydropower sold by the Department of Energy.

Saves $1 billion.

Ross Perot was right! Raising the gas tax 50 cents a gallon would slash the deficit while discouraging gas-guzzling. Start with a dime next year.

Raises $10 billion.

Maybe the saying should be: Nothing is certain except death *or* taxes. When an investor dies, his estate escapes the tax on capital gains. Close this loophole.

Raises $3 billion.

Increase the 24-cents-a-pack cigarette tax by $1 over the next four years. This would discourage teens from taking up this expensive, unhealthy habit.

Raises $3 billion.

End the right of oil, gas and some mineral firms to deduct a percentage of their gross income.

Raises $1 billion.

This is strong medicine. It is based on a premise that real deficit reduction will happen only if elected officials have the guts to tackle substantive areas of federal spending—not the relatively small pieces some are targeting now.

It is based on a premise that Americans will forgo tax cuts, close loopholes and absorb some higher taxes in service of fiscal responsibility.

It will mean pink slips for some bureaucrats, defense workers and others. It will require a spirit of shared sacrifice from those who have benefited most from the government's growing entitlements.

But the choice is simple: The harm of chronic deficits far outweighs the hurt from making government live within its means.

The Flat Tax: Alternative Views*

Alvin Rabushka

Robert E. Hall

ROBERT E. HALL AND ALVIN RABUSHKA

Simplify, Simplify

A surge of interest in complete reform of the Federal tax system is sweeping the country and energizing Washington. One source of the desire for change is disgust with the hideously complex tax system we now have. Another is the higher economic growth that a consumption tax would bring. And a third is the anger that honest taxpayers feel about widespread tax avoidance and tax evasion in the current system.

But the public also wants to retain one important feature of the existing system: progressivity, the principle that people with higher incomes should pay a higher percentage of that income in taxes. In particular, the poor should be exempt from tax up to a reasonable level of sustenance. The nation is ready for a simple, easily enforced, progressive tax on consumption.

For more than a decade, we have been advocating a tax reform with all of these features. Both the structure of the tax and estimates of its revenue have withstood close examination by experts, including the Treasury. The tax would reproduce the revenue of the current personal and corporate taxes with just a 19 percent rate. Our idea has generally been called the flat tax. But there is much more to it than just a simpler tax schedule.

One of the most important principles is to tax business income where it

*These articles appeared in the *New York Times* on February 8, 1995. Robert Hall and Alvin Rabushka are senior fellows at the Hoover Institution at Stanford. Robert Kuttner is co-editor of *The American Prospect*.

is generated—in businesses—rather than after it makes its way to individual taxpayers in the form of interest and dividends. Right now the system allows businesses to deduct such items, then tries to collect taxes from the recipients—an inefficient procedure that invites fraud.

To tax income at its source, we propose a comprehensive business tax. It would replace the current corporate income tax, personal taxes on noncorporate businesses and personal taxation of interest and dividends. Think of it as a withholding tax on interest, dividends and other types of income people earn from business. At the individual level, we'd tax only wages, salaries and pensions.

Here is where the system is progressive—a family of four pays tax only on earnings above an exemption level of $25,500. A family earning $25,000 pays no individual tax; one earning $50,000 pays $4,655, and one earning $100,000 pays $14,155. Dividends and interest have already been taxed at the business level and are not taxed again.

And the gains in simplicity are immense. Businesses and families can file their returns on forms the size of postcards. The numbers entered on these forms are clear and easy to calculate. Opportunities for evasion are minimized. The resources needed to comply with this streamlined tax system are a tiny fraction of those consumed today by Federal income taxes.

A family would pay a 19 percent tax on the amount that its wages, salaries and pensions exceed the exemption level. A business would pay a 19 percent tax on its revenue, with deductions for purchases of materials from other businesses; for its wages, salaries and pensions, and for its purchases of capital goods.

These deductions are central to the design of the tax. The deduction for materials bought from other businesses guarantees that business income is taxed once and only once. The deduction for wages, salaries and pensions recognizes that families pay taxes on these earnings. And the deduction for purchases of capital goods (plant and equipment) makes the tax a consumption tax.

Why do the family and business taxes add up to a consumption tax? Consumption is total income minus investment in new capital. Any tax imposed on income minus investment is a consumption tax.

There are many economically equivalent ways to administer a consumption tax. One obvious way would be a national sales tax on consumption of goods and services. The trick would be to make the sales tax progressive; that would require something like a family rebate of the tax on purchases up to an exemption level. But rebates create enormous opportunities for fraud. Even today, the Internal Revenue Service is battling a huge stream of fraudulent applications for tax refunds. The taxes we propose would be the equivalent of a 19 percent Federal sales tax together with a fraud-free rebate based on earnings.

Another way to set up a consumption tax is a value-added tax—the equivalent of a sales tax, collected along the way from businesses at every stage of production instead of the point where goods are sold to consumers. The entire tax is collected from businesses; individuals don't file tax returns. Value-added taxes are universal in Europe and have proved that broad taxes on consumption are feasible. But like a sales tax, a VAT is not progressive: it taxes a family's consumption from the first dollar. The only way to make it progressive is to issue rebates, and this opens the door for fraud.

The last way to set up a tax on consumption is to impose a tax on individuals, measuring consumption as what they earn minus what they save. Like our plan, the individual consumption tax is progressive without a rebate because it has a tax form for individuals and taxes are limited to the amount of consumption over an exemption level.

But an individual consumption tax would be an administrative nightmare. Not only would individuals have to report all types of income (rather than relying on universal withholding), but the IRS would have to keep track of billions of new items to measure saving. Dishonest taxpayers would overstate their payments into savings accounts and understate their withdrawals. True simplification and efficiency cannot be achieved with a family consumption tax.

Consider the goals we started with. Tax only consumption. Tax it progressively. Make it easy to comply and hard to commit fraud. The system embodied in our two post-card-sized forms is the unique proposal that delivers them all.

The Flat Tax: Alternative Views

ROBERT KUTTNER

Instead, Close Loopholes

Tax all business and personal income at a flat rate, say 17 or 19 percent. Eliminate all deductions, depreciation schedules and other complications. Raise the personal exemption, so moderate-income households pay little or no tax. It sounds wonderful.

But on closer examination, the logic of such "flat tax" plans falls apart. Behind the promise of simplicity and tax reduction are higher deficits and a more regressive tax system.

The leading proposal on the table right now is by Representative Richard Armey of Texas, the House majority leader. As drafted, it would cost the Treasury more than $200 billion a year. To be truly revenue-neutral, it would require a rate of more than 25 percent, increasing taxes on all but the wealthiest payers.

The silliest part of the "flat tax" notion is the very premise that simplification requires a single rate. Tax rates, of course, are not what makes taxation complex. For individuals and businesses, calculating the rate is the easy part. Whether the schedule is flat or graduated, you just multiply taxable income by the applicable rate. The complicated part is figuring out what constitutes taxable income—what should be deducted, if anything, before you calculate your taxes.

Eliminating deductions would obviously simplify the tax system. But some tax preferences, like the mortgage interest deduction, serve good social purposes, and others, like the deduction for medical expenses, reflect

146

the fact that if you earn $60,000 and have to spend $30,000 on doctor and hospital bills, you don't have the same resources as a healthy person who makes $60,000. Mr. Armey would do away with both.

Businesses' taxable income, likewise, is no simple matter to calculate. If we swept away the complex treatment of business income and expenses, a lot of businesses would be taxed on their expenses as well as their profits.

The more serious mischief in the flat tax campaign is the tired claim that we can have a free lunch: lower taxes for most people and no effect on the budget. Mr. Armey says this is possible since "as the economy grows because of the favorable treatment of savings, investment and low marginal tax rates, revenue to the Treasury will grow."

If this sounds familiar, it's because under its old name—supply-side economics—it was discredited by a full field test in the 1980s. Ronald Reagan's supply-side tax cuts never delivered their promised revenue increases; deficits became chronic and the national debt tripled. Conversely, during the long postwar boom, rates on the richest taxpayers were as high as 91 percent and the economy did just fine. And ever since the top tax rate was raised in the 1993 budget accord, the economy has been growing at least 4 percent a year.

The Treasury Department calculated last fall that far from raising more money, a flat tax of 17 percent would reduce tax receipts by $244 billion a year. Mr. Armey complained that the Treasury had misunderstood certain technical aspects of the bill, such as the interaction of income and payroll taxes. Treasury disagreed, but found that even accepting Mr. Armey's technical adjustments, the plan would still lose $186 billion a year.

An analysis by Citizens for Tax Justice, based on the Treasury findings, calculates that a revenue-neutral version of the Armey plan would require a flat rate of 25.8 percent. That would mean higher taxes for every income group—except people making $200,000 or more. That group would enjoy an average tax cut of $28,410.

Mr. Armey's plan, like other such proposals, was inspired by the economists Robert Hall and Alvin Rabushka, whose 1983 book *Low Tax, Simple Tax* promised similar miracles (with similar mathematical ingenuity). But even Mr. Hall has been quoted as estimating that the Armey plan would require a 23 percent tax rate to break even; and the Hall-Rabushka book acknowledged that a flat tax would be "a tremendous boon to the economic elite" and that "lower taxes on the successful will have to be made up by higher taxes on average people."

The tax system can be greatly simplified without giving up graduated rates. The 1986 Tax Reform Act, sponsored by Representative Richard Gephardt of Missouri and Senator Bill Bradley of New Jersey, cut rates top and bottom, and paid for the cuts by closing loopholes. President Clinton's

1993 tax amendments paid for tax relief at the bottom by raising rates at the top.

There are still plenty of loopholes that don't make economic sense. Large inheritances are so shielded from taxes that the estate tax is mostly, as a Brookings Institution study dryly termed it, "voluntary." Tax breaks for second homes and lavish deductions of business expenses can be eliminated to cut taxes on working families.

Nobody likes taxes. But if we are to have public services at all, it makes sense to pay for them by taxing wealthy people at higher rates than the middle and working class. Mr. Gephardt, now the House minority leader, recently proposed that by closing additional loopholes, we could reduce rates and yet retain a system at least as progressive as the current one. The Gephardt approach has been described in some quarters as a Democratic flat tax, yet another case of Democrats embracing Republican ideas. It is not. It is a marriage of tax simplification and tax fairness—without raiding the Treasury.

The very idea of a flat tax is a reversal of the well-established principle of taxation based on ability to pay. Progressive taxation dates to Woodrow Wilson. It is sensible economics, popular politics and sound fiscal policy. Democrats would make a big mistake to borrow the "flat tax" concept—or the label.

QUESTIONS FOR ANALYSIS

1. Peter Peterson argues that to increase productivity, we must invest much more, which means we must save more. Why?

2. To save more, Peterson says that we should reduce and eventually eliminate the federal deficit. Why?

3. To reduce the deficit, Peterson contends that entitlements like Social Security and Medicare must be cut. In his view, the problem is that "[a]ll of us have decided that we are *entitled* to much more than our society can afford to pay for . . ." Do you agree? Why or why not?

4. *Business Week* and the *Philadelphia Inquirer* agree on a considerable number of cuts that should be made in federal spending. What are these areas of agreement?

5. *Business Week* and the *Philadelphia Inquirer* do not agree on a variety of cuts that might be made in federal spending. What are the areas of disagreement?

6. Is it really necessary that the United States reduce its budget deficit? Why or why not?

7. Are spending cuts the only way to reduce the deficit? If not, what other ways are there?

8. Professors Hall and Rabushka argue for a tax on consumption expenditure, not on income. What are the advantages of such a tax?

9. Mr. Kuttner argues strongly for progressive taxation—that is, for the principle that tax rates should be higher for the affluent than for the poor. Do Professors Hall and Rabushka reject this argument?

10. According to Professors Hall and Rabushka, their form of a flat tax is preferable to a value-added tax. Why?

PART EIGHT

MONETARY

POLICY

In the mid-1990s, there was considerable and continuous controversy over monetary policy. Many observers believed that the Federal Reserve's policies were not sufficiently expansionary; others felt that the opposite was true. The first article in this part is the testimony of Alan Greenspan, chairman of the Fed, before the House Banking Committee in 1993. The second article is an attack on the policies announced in Greenspan's testimony by Henry Gonzalez, chairman of the House Banking Committee. The third article, by Alan Blinder, discusses what the Federal Reserve's objectives should be.

The Fed Aims for Price Stability

ALAN GREENSPAN*

Thank you for this opportunity to discuss the Federal Reserve's semi-annual monetary policy report to the Congress. My remarks this morning will cover the current monetary policy and economic settings, as well as the Federal Reserve's longer-term strategy for contributing, to the best of our abilities, to the nation's economic well-being.

As the economic expansion has progressed somewhat fitfully, our earlier characterization of the economy as facing stiff headwinds has appeared increasingly appropriate. Doubtless the major headwind in this regard has been the combined efforts of households, businesses, and financial institutions to repair and to rebuild their balance sheets following the damage inflicted in recent years as weakening asset values exposed excessive debt burdens.

But there have been other headwinds as well. The build-down of national defense has cast a shadow over particular industries and regions of the country. Spending on nonresidential real estate dropped dramatically in the face of overbuilding and high vacancy rates, and has remained in the doldrums. At the same time, corporations across a wide range of industries have been making efforts to pare employment and expenses in order to im-

*Alan Greenspan is chairman of the Board of Governors of the Federal Reserve System. This testimony was presented before the Committee on Banking, Finance, and Urban Affairs of the U.S. House of Representatives on July 20, 1993.

prove productivity and their competitive positions. These efforts have been prompted in part by innovative technologies, which have been applied to almost every area of economic endeavor, and have boosted investment. However, their effect on jobs and wages through much of the expansion also has made households more cautious spenders.

In the past several years, as these influences have restrained the economy, they have been balanced in part by the accommodative stance of monetary policy and, more recently, by declines in longer-term interest rates as the prospects for credible federal deficit cuts improved. From the time monetary policy began to move toward ease in 1989 to now, short-term interest rates have dropped by more than two-thirds and long-term rates have declined substantially too. All along the maturity spectrum, interest rates have come down to their lowest levels in twenty or thirty years, aiding the repair of balance sheets, bolstering the cash flow of borrowers, and providing support for interest-sensitive spending.

The process of easing monetary policy, however, had to be closely controlled and generally gradual, because of the constraint imposed by the marketplace's acute sensitivity to inflation. As I pointed out in my February testimony to the Congress, this is a constraint that did not exist in an earlier time. Before the late 1970s, financial market participants and others apparently believed that, while inflationary pressures might surface from time to time, the institutional structure of the U.S. economy simply would not permit sustained inflation. But as inflation and, consequently, long-term interest rates soared into the double digits at the end of the 1970s, investors became painfully aware that they had underestimated the economy's potential for inflation. As a result, monetary policy in recent years has had to remain alert to the possibility that an ill-timed easing could be undone by a flare-up of inflation expectations, pushing long-term interest rates higher, and short-circuiting essential balance sheet repair.

The cumulative monetary easing over the last four years has been very substantial. Since last September, however, no further steps have been taken, as the stance of policy has appeared broadly appropriate to the evolving economic circumstances.

That stance has been quite accommodative, especially judging by the level of real short-term interest rates in the context of, on average, moderate economic growth. Short-term real interest rates have been in the neighborhood of zero over the last three quarters. In maintaining this accommodative stance, we have been persuaded by the evidence of persistent slack in labor and product markets, increasing international competitiveness, and the decided absence of excessive credit and money expansion. The forces that engendered past inflationary episodes appear to have been lacking to date.

DISTURBING INDICATIONS OF INFLATION

Yet some of the readings on inflation earlier this year were disturbing. It appeared that prices might be accelerating despite product market slack and an unemployment rate noticeably above estimates of the so-called "natural" rate of unemployment—that is, the rate at which price pressures remain roughly constant. In the past, the existing degree of slack in the economy had been consistent with continuing disinflation.

However, the inflation outcome, history tells us, depends not only on the amount of slack remaining in labor and product markets, but on other factors as well, including the rate at which that slack is changing. If the economy is growing rapidly, inflation pressures can arise, even in the face of excess capacity, as temporary bottlenecks emerge and as workers and producers raise wages and prices in anticipation of continued strengthening in demand. Near the end of last year, about the time many firms probably were finalizing their plans for 1993, sales and capacity utilization were moving up markedly and there was a surge of optimism about future economic activity. This may well have set in motion a wave of price increases, which showed through to broad measures of prices earlier this year.

Moreover, inflation expectations, at least by some measures, appear to have tilted upward this year, possibly contributing to price pressures. The University of Michigan survey of consumer attitudes, for example, reported an increase in the inflation rate expected to prevail over the next 12 months from about 3.75 percent in the fourth quarter of last year to nearly 4.5 percent in the second quarter of this year. Preliminary data imply some easing of such expectations earlier this month, but the sample from which those data are derived is too small to be persuasive. Moreover, the price of gold, which can be broadly reflective of inflationary expectations, has risen sharply in recent months. And at times this spring, bond yields spiked higher when incoming news about inflation was most discouraging.

The role of expectations in the inflation process is crucial. Even expectations not validated by economic fundamentals can themselves add appreciably to wage and price pressures for a considerable period, potentially derailing the economy from its growth track.

Why, for example, despite an above-normal rate of unemployment and permanent layoffs, have uncertainties about job security not led to further moderation in wage increases? The answer appears to lie, at least in part, in the deep-seated anticipations understandably harbored by workers that inflation is likely to reaccelerate in the near term and undercut their real wages.

The Federal Open Market Committee (FOMC) became concerned that inflation expectations and price pressures, unless contained, could raise long-term interest rates and stall economic expansion. Consequently, at its meeting in May, while affirming the more accommodative policy stance in place since last September, the FOMC also deemed it appropriate to initiate a so-called asymmetric directive. Such a directive, with its bias in the direction of a possible firming of policy over the inter-meeting period, does not prejudge that action will be taken—and indeed none occurred. But it did indicate that further signs of a potential deterioration of the inflation outlook would merit serious consideration of whether short-term rates needed to be raised slightly from their relatively low levels to ensure that financial conditions remained conducive to sustained growth.

Certainly the May and June price figures have helped assuage concerns that new inflationary pressures had taken hold. Nonetheless, on balance, the news on inflation this year must be characterized as disappointing. Despite disinflationary forces and continued slack, the rate of inflation has, at best, stabilized, rather than easing further as past relationships would have suggested.

In assessing the stance of monetary policy and the likelihood of persistent inflationary pressures, the FOMC took account of the downshift in the pace of economic expansion earlier this year. This downshift left considerable remaining slack in the economy and promised that the adverse price movements prompted by the acceleration in growth late last year likely would deminish. . .

Over the last two years, the forces of restraint on the economy have changed, but real growth has continued, with one sector of the economy after another taking the lead. Against this background, Federal Reserve Board governors and Reserve Bank presidents project that the U.S. economy will remain on the moderate growth path it has been following as the expansion has progressed. Their forecasts for real GDP average around 2.5 percent from the fourth quarter of 1992 to the fourth quarter of 1993, and cluster around 2.5 to 3.25 percent over the four quarters of 1994. Reflecting this moderate rise and the outlook for labor productivity, unemployment is generally expected to edge lower, to around 6.75 percent by the end of this year, and to perhaps a shade lower by the end of next year. For this year as a whole, FOMC participants see inflation at or just above 3 percent, and most of them have the same forecast for next year.

In addition to focusing on the outlook for the economy at its July meeting, the FOMC, as required by the Humphrey-Hawkins Act, set ranges for the growth of money and debt for this year, and, on a preliminary basis, for 1994. One premise of the discussion of the ranges was that the uncharacteristically slow growth of the broad monetary aggregates in the last couple of years—and the atypical increases in their velocities—would persist for a while longer. M_2 has been far weaker than income and interest rates would predict. Indeed, if the historical relationships between M_2 and nominal income had remained intact, the behavior of M_2 in recent years would have been consistent with an economy in severe contraction. To an important degree, the behavior of M_2 has reflected structural changes in the financial sector: The thrift industry has downsized by necessity, and commercial banks have pulled back as well, largely reflecting the burgeoning loan losses that followed the lax lending of earlier years. With depository credit weak, there has been little bidding for deposits, and depositors, in any case, have been drawn to the higher returns on capital market instruments. Inflows to bond and stock mutual funds have reached record levels, and, to the extent that these inflows have come at the expense of growth in deposits or money-market mutual funds, the broad monetary aggregates have been depressed.

In this context, the FOMC lowered the 1993 ranges for M_2 and M_3 to 1-to-5 percent and 0-to-4 percent, respectively. This represents a reduction of one percentage point in the M_2 range and a half percentage point for M_3. Even with these reductions, we would not be surprised to see the monetary aggregates finish the year near the lower ends of their ranges.

MONETARY AGGREGATE ESTIMATES NO LONGER RELIABLE

As I emphasized in a similar context in February, the lowering of the ranges is purely a technical matter; it does not indicate, nor should it be perceived as, a shift of monetary policy in the direction of restraint. It is indicative merely of the state of our knowledge about the factors depressing the growth of the aggregates relative to spending, of the course of the aggregates to date, and of the likelihood of various outcomes through the end of the year. While the lowering of the range reflects our judgment that shifts out of M_2 will persist, the upper end of the revised range allows for a resumption of more normal behavior, or even some unwinding of M_2 shortfalls. The FOMC also lowered the 1993 range for debt of the domestic nonfinancial sectors, by a half percentage point, to 4-to-8 percent. The debt aggregate is likely to come in comfortably within its new range, as it continues growing about in line with nominal GDP. The new ranges for growth of money and debt in 1993 were carried over on a preliminary basis into 1994.

In reading the longer-run intentions of the FOMC, the specific ranges need to be interpreted cautiously. The historical relationships between money and income, and between money and the price level, have largely broken down, depriving the aggregates of much of their usefulness as guides to policy. At least for the time being, M_2 has been downgraded as a reliable indicator of financial conditions in the economy, and no single variable has yet been identified to take its place. . .

In these circumstances, it is especially prudent to focus on longer-term policy guides. One important guidepost is real interest rates, which have a key bearing on longer-run spending decisions and inflation prospects.

In assessing real rates, the central issue is their relationship to an equilibrium interest rate, specifically the real rate level that, if maintained, would keep the economy at its production potential over time. Rates persisting above that level, history tells us, tend to be associated with slack, disinflation, and economic stagnation—below that level with eventual resource bottlenecks and rising inflation, which ultimately engenders economic contraction. Maintaining the real rate around its equilibrium level should have a stabilizing effect on the economy, directing production toward its long-term potential.

The level of the equilibrium real rate—or, more appropriately, the equilibrium term structure of real rates—cannot be estimated with a great deal of confidence, though with enough to be useful for monetary policy. Real rates, of course, are not directly observable, but must be inferred from nominal interest rates and estimates of inflation expectations. The most important real rates for private spending decisions almost surely are the longer maturities. Moreover, the equilibrium rate structure responds to the ebb and flow of underlying forces affecting spending. So, for example, in recent years, the appropriate real rate structure doubtless has been depressed by the headwinds of balance sheet restructuring and fiscal retrenchment. Despite the uncertainties about the levels of equilibrium and actual real interest rates, rough judgments about these variables can be made and used in conjunction with other indicators in the monetary policy process. Currently, short-term real rates, most directly affected by the Federal Reserve, are not far from zero; long-term rates, set primarily by the market, are appreciably higher, judging from the steep slope of the yield curve and reasonable suppositions about inflation expectations. This configuration indicates that market participants anticipate that short-term real rates will have to rise as the headwinds diminish, if substantial inflationary imbalances are to be avoided. . .

I believe we are on our way toward reestablishing the trust in the purchasing power of the dollar that is crucial to maximizing and fulfilling the productivity capacity of this nation. The public, however, clearly remains to be convinced: Survey responses and financial market prices embody expectations that the current lower level of inflation not only will not be bettered, it will not even persist. But there are glimmers of hope that trust is reemerging. For example, issuers have found receptive markets in recent months for fifty-year bonds. This had not happened in decades. The re-opening of that market may be read as one indication that some investors once again believe that inflationary pressures will remain subdued.

It is my firm belief that, with fiscal consolidation and with the monetary policy path that we have charted, the United States is well-positioned to re-main at the forefront of the world economy well into the next century.

An Open Letter to the President

HENRY B. GONZALEZ*

Dear President Clinton:

I am very disappointed with Federal Reserve Chairman Alan Greenspan's announcement Tuesday [July 20] that the Federal Reserve will ratchet down the targets for money growth from 2 to 6 percent to 1 to 5 percent. The Federal Reserve has failed to meet its own targets for a year and a half, and now is moving the targets down to actual recession levels of money growth. With new reports that the industrial sector actually shrunk in June and consumer confidence fell, a policy that allows one percent growth in our nation's money supply will cause continued hardship for our nation's workers and families.

The Federal Reserve decision-makers have lowered their range for the projected real Gross Domestic Product (GDP) growth in 1993 from their February 1993 estimate of 2.5 to 4.0 percent, to their new estimate of 2.0 to 3.5 percent. Slow growth of 2.0 to 2.5 percent is within their projected plans.

Instead of this continued policy of virtually no growth, this is the time to urge the Federal Reserve to follow a monetary policy that is consistent with your policies to put our citizens back to work. The money supply (defined

*Henry B. Gonzalez was chairman of the Committee on Banking, Finance, and Urban Affairs of the U.S. House of Representatives. He wrote this letter on July 22, 1993.

160

as M_2) should be growing at least as fast as the production of goods and services in a full employment economy. A growth rate of 4.5 percent for M_2 falls in the middle of the Federal Reserve's money supply target range for 1992 and would be appropriate. With the economy stagnating as it is, a small increase in the money supply is not enough to reignite inflation.

I urge you to consider changing the composition of the Federal Open Market Committee (FOMC) which decides our nation's monetary policies. The current Federal Reserve decision-makers are seven Reagan-Bush appointees at the Board of Governors. The twelve Federal Reserve presidents are selected by their Bank board of directors, who mostly represent commercial banks.

In general, the Federal Reserve decision-makers are bankers or friends of bankers. Decision-makers representing the concerns of agriculture, small business, labor, consumer, and community groups are almost unheard of. Yet advocates of price stability even at the price of stagnation are well-represented at the FOMC.

It is long past time to change the Federal Reserve's inbred network by appointing people who are competent in central bank policy, including monetary policy. There are many competent women and minorities who never get a chance to serve on the FOMC because they cannot rise up through the old boy's bank network. Competency—not who you know in the banking world, and the ability to think for yourself and not just to march in lockstep—should top the list of requirements for being selected to the FOMC. I know that you have sought diversity and competence when making appointments in your administration, and I applaud you for that.

When Governor Wayne D. Angell's term expires on January 31, 1994, you will have the opportunity to put a different face on the Federal Reserve. Your nominee could achieve considerable clout. Not only will he or she serve as a Federal Reserve Governor, the nominee could also become the board's vice-chairman when David W. Mullins, Jr.'s term as vice-chairman ends July 24, 1995. Although Governor Mullins's term as governor does not end until January 31, 1996, you will have to select the vice-chairman in 1995 from among the sitting governors.

Last week, the Fed selected one of their own, William J. McDonough, as president of the New York Federal Reserve Bank. Mr. McDonough's qualifications and his views on monetary policy, on zero inflation, on regulation of the banking industry, and on consumer issues, will not be debated in public. His expertise in central bank monetary policy will not be questioned in Senate confirmation hearings. However, because he has been selected through the Federal Reserve's internal private mechanisms, he will manage our nation's money supply without ever going before the American people or their representatives.

I urge you to consider changing the law so that the twelve Federal Reserve Bank presidents would be appointed by the President and approved by the Senate, as is currently the case with candidates for Federal Reserve Governor. Because monetary policy is so crucial to the economy's well-being, it is essential that the public have some say over who will be controlling the money supply which affects inflation, employment, interest rates, and the international value of our currency. Meanwhile, I again respectfully urge you to encourage the Federal Reserve to follow policies more consistent with a reasonable level of growth. This can be done without reigniting inflation, whereas current policies are certain to lead to continued stagnation, decline, and hardships for millions who look to you for hope, and for change.

Sincerely,

Henry B. Gonzalez, Chairman

Reflections of a Central Banker

ALAN BLINDER*

I am here today in a very new role for me. While I am not young by any reasonable criterion, I am very young as a central banker. I've been here at the Kansas City Fed conferences in Jackson Hole several times before, but always as an academic speaker, where my role was clearly to say something and maybe even to say something interesting. It is quite clear that, in my new job, my new role is to say nothing and certainly not to say anything interesting.

Mindful of that dictum, I'd like to take us back to the perspective of a central banker, which is to say back to macroeconomics—a subject we haven't talked about very much in the symposium in general, but especially not this morning. (That is not criticism at all; I feel it was quite appropriate to discuss the things we have discussed this morning.) In particular, I was very glad to see, when I received the program, that this is a conference about *reducing*, not *increasing*, unemployment. Charts 18 and 19 (eight panels in all) illustrate what a woman from Mars who landed here in Jackson Hole to look at the unemployment history of the world since 1970 would have seen: the standardized (by the Organization for Economic Cooperation and Development [OECD]) unemployment rates of a nonrandomly

*This is an excerpt from a paper presented at a symposium at Jackson Hole, Wyoming, on August 27, 1994. Alan Blinder is vice-chairman of the Board of Governors of the Federal Reserve System.

CHART 18   Standardized Unemployment Rates

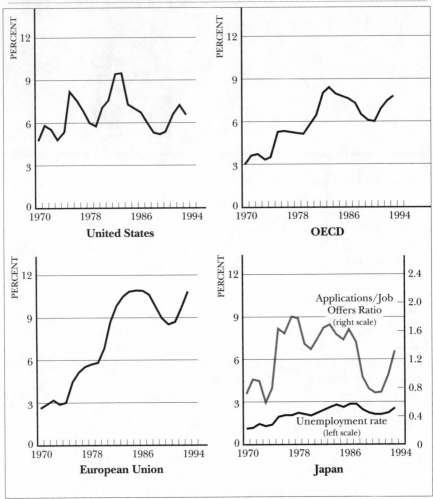

Sources: OECD Main Economic Indicators.

selected sample. The eight panels cover every country represented on the program—including the OECD and the European Union as countries—except, I'm sorry to say, New Zealand. That's because the OECD does not have a standardized unemployment rate for New Zealand that goes back this far. So this is the entire available sample. The hypothetical woman from Mars could be forgiven for wondering if the governments of these countries were really worrying about *reducing* unemployment during this

CHART 19 Standardized Unemployment Rates

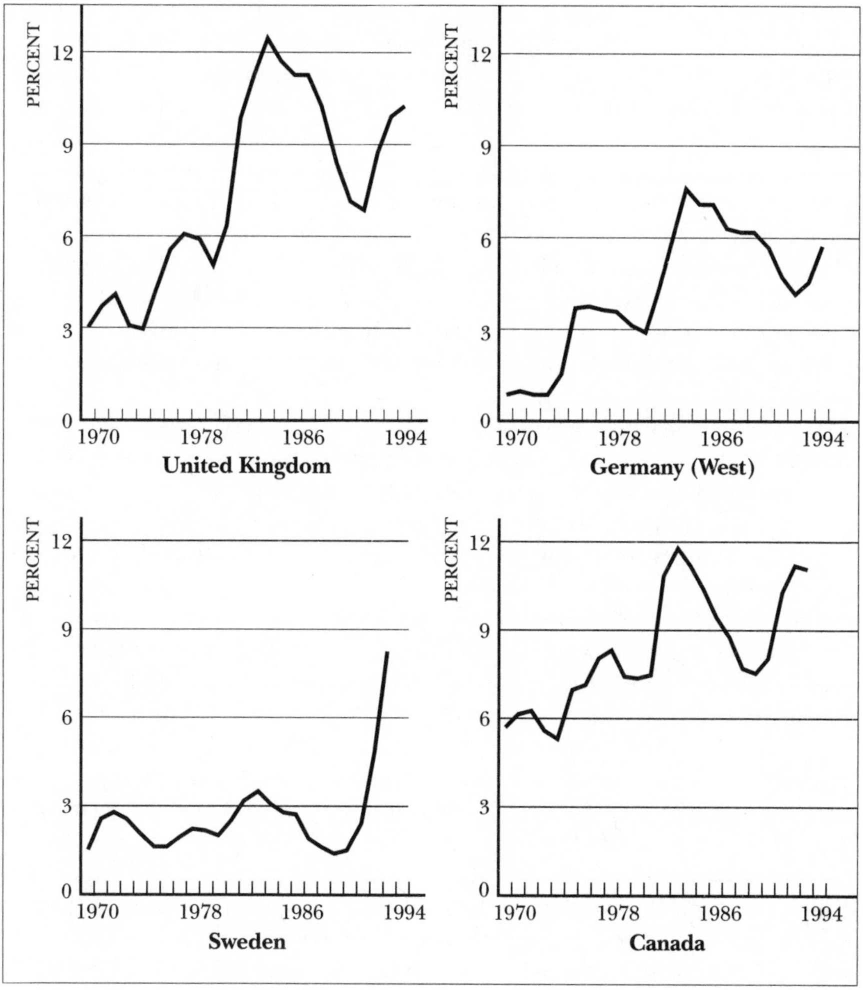
PERCENT
12
9
6
3
0
1970
1978
1986
1994
United Kingdom
Germany (West)
Sweden
Canada

Sources: OECD Main Economic Indicators.

period rather than *increasing* unemployment. If they were worrying about reducing it, they weren't doing too well—except perhaps for Japan and the United States.

Now, in my view, central banks, or more generally macroeconomic policies, do indeed have a role in reducing unemployment as well as, not incidentally, in reducing inflation. Before I pursue that point further, there is a preliminary point—actually a hurdle which, if not jumped, leaves nothing more to say on the subject. That hurdle is this: for a central bank to have any role in either raising or reducing unemployment, you have to believe in Keynesianism. If you don't, changes in aggregate demand are all dissipated in prices right away—up or down—and you just don't have any ability to affect the unemployment rate.

The *Fortune Encyclopedia of Economics* has a definition of Keynesian economics. I wrote it, so I know what's in it. I am only going to summarize the first half of it, which is the definition of *positive* Keynesianism, forgetting about any *normative* considerations. This definition has three pieces, and I'll just read them briefly. First, it says: "A Keynesian believes that aggregate demand is influenced by a host of economic decisions—both public and private—and sometimes behaves erratically. The public decisions include, most prominently, those on monetary and fiscal (i.e., spending and tax) policy."

Second, it says that a Keynesian believes that: ". . . changes in aggregate demand, whether anticipated or unanticipated, have their greatest short-run impact on real output and employment, not on prices."

And third: "Keynesians believe that prices and, especially, wages respond slowly to changes in supply and demand, resulting in shortages and surpluses, especially of labor."

That is at least one person's definition of what it means to be Keynesian, in a positive sense. Now, by this definition, I submit that President Nixon had it right when he said, "We are all Keynesians now." (I think he said this in the 1970s.) Money is not neutral, and I don't think I have to take any time to defend that proposition any longer—although I must say that, if this were a conference of academics, I probably would. If you accept this proposition, then I can go on. If you don't, of course, I can sit down right now. (I suppose I shouldn't put that to a vote!)

If you accept this proposition and you accept the natural rate hypothesis, which has been thoroughly discussed at this meeting, they lead to what I like to call "the approximate dichotomy." I'll come at the end to why it is only "approximate"—or at least one reason why—but this is what I mean by the approximate dichotomy: where employment is concerned, in the short run macroeconomics is everything and in the long run macroeconomics is nothing.

Let me elaborate slightly on what I mean by that. In the short run, changes in aggregate demand can and do easily change the unemployment rate by, say, plus or minus two percentage points. Such events happen frequently in business cycles. There is nothing, I submit, that we know in the way of microeconomic interventions that could have an effect remotely close to that in the United States—certainly not in the short run, and maybe not even in the long run. So that's one-half of the dichotomy.

However, in the long run the meaning of the natural rate hypothesis, as Dale Mortensen stated clearly this morning, is that the unemployment rate will converge to the natural rate *regardless of macroeconomic policy*. And that means, roughly speaking, that the employment rate of five to ten years from now has nothing to do with today's macroeconomic policy. The latter is totally irrelevant. Today's macroeconomic policy will, however, have something to do with the price level of five to ten years from now.

I emphasize this dichotomy because, while it is mother's milk to economists, it is almost totally unknown outside the economics profession—indeed it is a totally foreign doctrine. Very few people have in their heads the notion that the effects of aggregate demand on jobs are temporary, which is not to say ephemeral—I don't mean they are gone in three to six months, they are certainly not—but temporary. Nor do most people realize that a very big microeconomic achievement, at least in the United States, might be reducing the natural rate of unemployment by 0.25 percent. That would be a major, major achievement. But I think that very few people outside the economics profession understand either part of this dichotomy, which is a shame.

In view of this approximate dichotomy, what is a poor central banker to do? My view is that we should remember a television quiz show that I occasionally watched in my wasted youth called *The Price Is Right*. You may remember that on *The Price Is Right* an object would appear, and contestants were supposed to guess the price. You won if you came as close to the actual price as possible *without going over*. That was the name of the game. Similarly, in my view, the job of a central bank, in this regard, is to guide the employment rate up to its natural rate, but not higher than that. By that criterion, I think the United States is extremely close to being "on target," but the European Union, I believe, is quite far from being on target.

I have stated quite clearly, I think, that I believe the central bank does have a role in reducing unemployment, or raising employment. But, as we know, not all central banks explicitly recognize an employment objective of that sort. We heard very eloquently at lunch yesterday, from Mr. Brash, the virtues of single-minded concentration on an inflation, or a price level, objective. The charge given by the Congress to the Federal Reserve is quite different, as many of you know. It calls upon us to pursue *both* maximum employment *and* stable prices. Since these two objectives conflict in the short run, the Federal Reserve Act calls upon us to strike a balance. That has always seemed very appropriate to me.

In thinking about the fact that different central banks have quite different stated objectives, I started to wonder whether the objectives actually matter. And, while I was wondering about that, I stumbled upon something which some of you have seen before: a ranking of central banks by Alex

Cukierman and two coauthors. (See Chart 20.) Cukierman *et al.* rated 21 industrial countries by what they called "central bank independence." Actually, I think this was quite a big misnomer because, if you notice, the United States is ranked pretty low. And I can tell you we feel fairly independent at the Fed, at least inside the building. In fact, the rankings really rate central banks on the singlemindedness of their concentration on inflation reduction, or price-level stability. Here, again, I must apologize to New Zealand. I didn't make up these rankings, and they came before the Reserve Bank Act of 1989. New Zealand, among other countries, would clearly be ranked differently today.

What I've done in Chart 20 is looked at the period of disinflation: 1980–1993. It seems to me that around 1980 the countries of the industrialized world looked back at the 1970s and said: "Enough—indeed, too much. We had an awful lot of inflation, it didn't do anybody any good, and we ought to get rid of it." There was a kind of sea change in attitudes around the world, although not with exactly the same timing everywhere.

So Chart 20 examines the period between 1980 and 1993. Central banks are ranked by the objective index created by Cukierman *et al.,* with 1.0 connoting the most single-minded concentration on inflation reduction—you see, for example, that the Bundesbank is on the far right on this criterion—and with zero on the other extreme: banks that did not have any inflation objective at all in their charge (that includes the Bank of Japan and it included then, but not now, the Bank of France). And the question I asked was: Did the bank's legally stated objective make any difference to what happened in this 13-year period? Was there any systematic difference between the banks that were focused on inflation reduction and those that were not?

Well, the top panel shows the changes in inflation over that period. You can see that it is negative for every one of these countries; this was, after all, a period of disinflation. But the answer to the question is no. There is no correlation . . . between how much inflation fell and the legal charge of the central bank.

The lower panel shows that there was some correlation—not overwhelming, but noticeable—between the rise in unemployment and the central bank's objective. . . . So unemployment rose in every one of these countries, essentially; and it rose more in the countries whose central banks were more singlemindedly devoted to inflation reduction. But the difference is not tremendously significant. The message, I think, may be that the significance of the central bank's charge may be more apparent than real. But I wouldn't dismiss it entirely. Now, there is a two-handed answer for you!

CHART 20   Central Bank Objectives, Inflation, and Unemployment

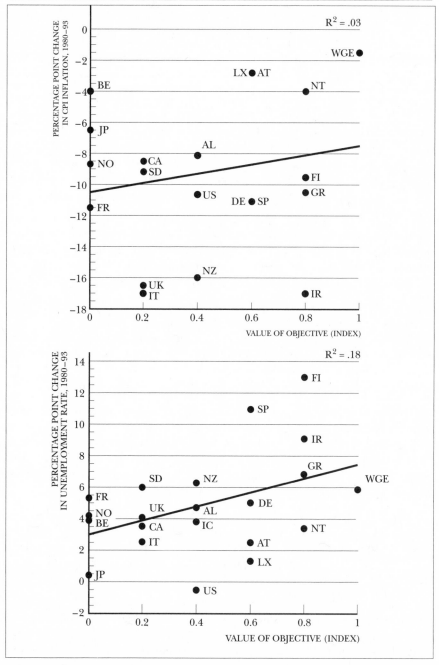

Source: A. Cukierman, S. Webb, and B. Neyapti, "Measuring the Independence of Central Banks and Its Effect on Policy Outcomes," *World Bank Economic Review* 6,3 (September 1992) 353–398.

QUESTIONS FOR ANALYSIS

1. Why all the fuss about the money supply? What problems arise if the money supply grows too slowly? What problems arise if it grows too fast?

2. What is the money supply? Both Dr. Greenspan and Mr. Gonzalez refer to M_2. What is M_2?

3. Dr. Greenspan testified that: "The historical relationships between money and income, and between money and the price level, have largely broken down, depriving the aggregates of much of their usefulness as guides to policy. At least for the time being, M_2 has been downgraded as a reliable indicator of financial conditions in the economy, and no single variable has yet been identified to take its place." How then can the Federal Reserve conduct monetary policy? If you were a member of the Federal Open Market Committee, how would you figure out whether money and credit should be tightened or loosened?

4. Mr. Gonzalez protests the Federal Reserve's lowering of the targets for money growth from 2 to 6 percent to 1 to 5 percent. In his view, "The money supply (defined as M_2) should be growing at least as fast as the production of goods and services in a full employment economy." Why do you think that he believes this to be true? Do you agree? Why or why not?

5. Dr. Greenspan, concerned about inflationary pressures, says: "I believe we are on our way toward reestablishing the trust in the purchasing power of the dollar that is crucial to maximizing and fulfilling the productivity capacity of this nation." Why does he feel that it is so important to reestablish the trust in the purchasing power of the dollar? Do you agree with him? Why or why not?

6. In Dr. Greenspan's view, inflationary expectations have not been quelled. "Survey responses and financial market prices embody expectations that the current lower level of inflation not only will not be bettered, it will not even persist." Why is he so concerned about expectations? Isn't reality what is important, not expectations? How can the economy be hurt or threatened by something as ephemeral and hard-to-measure as expectations?

7. The real interest rate equals the interest rate minus the inflation rate. Dr. Greenspan says that short-term real interest rates, the interest rates "most directly affected by the Federal Reserve, are not far from zero." Why is the real interest rate of importance to policy makers? If the real interest rate is zero, does this indicate that money is easy or tight? Why?

8. According to Mr. Gonzalez, "With the economy stagnating as it is, a small increase in the money supply is not enough to reignite inflation." In what respects was the economy "stagnating" in July 1993? Contrast Mr. Gonzalez's views of the state of the economy and the likelihood of serious inflation with those of Mr. Greenspan.

9. In making decisions regarding monetary policy, must the Federal Reserve be concerned about the position and slope of the short-run aggregate supply curve? If so, why? If not, why not?

10. Mr. Gonzalez urged President Clinton "to consider changing the composition of the Federal Open Market Committee (FOMC) which decides our nation's monetary policies . . . [A]dvocates of price stability even at the price of stagnation are well-represented at the FOMC." Must we tolerate more inflation in order to reduce unemployment? Will inflation necessarily increase employment and output? Do you agree that the composition of the FOMC should be changed?

11. Subsequently, Alan Blinder of Princeton University, and Janet Yellen of the University of California at Berkeley, were appointed by President Clinton to the Federal Reserve Board. In late 1994, Dr. Blinder, vice-chairman of the board, made some remarks indicating that he would be less likely to increase interest rates when unemployment is high. An uproar resulted, after which he is reported to have said, "If you are on a central bank board, you ought to keep your mouth shut."* Do you agree with his original remarks? Why or why not? Do you agree that he ought to keep his mouth shut? Why or why not?

12. In late October, data issued by the U.S. Department of Commerce indicated that, in the third quarter of 1994, GDP grew at an annual rate of 3.4 percent, well in excess of the 2.5 percent growth rate that many people regarded as the maximum that could occur without causing increased inflation. (Recall pages 121–27). On November 15, the Federal Open Market Committee raised the discount rate by 3/4 percentage point. Why?

13. What does Dr. Blinder have in mind when he says that "the effects of aggregate demand on jobs are temporary"?

14. Do you agree with Dr. Blinder that "the significance of the central bank's charge may be more apparent than real"? Why or why not?

*New York Times, September 11, 1994, p. 2F.

PART NINE

INTERNATION-AL TRADE POLICY

The mid-1990s have seen a great deal of controversy over U.S. trade policy. Some influential political leaders and industrialists feel strongly that we should engage in "managed trade"; others disagree—equally strongly. The first article is by Paul Krugman of Stanford University who argues that the alleged competitiveness problem of the United States is greatly exaggerated. The second article is by Robert A. Lutz, president of the Chrysler Corporation, who favors managed trade. The third article is by Robert T. Parry, president of the Federal Reserve Bank of San Francisco, who opposes managed trade.

The Fixation on Competitiveness

PAUL KRUGMAN*

In the movie *The Music Man,* Robert Preston plays a traveling salesman who specializes in selling musical instruments and uniforms for marching bands to small towns. To make his sale in River City, he needs to convince local leaders that they have a problem he can solve. And so he manages to turn the formerly innocuous pool hall into a symbol of gathering social danger, to which the answer is, of course, the healthy town spirit that only a properly equipped school band can provide.

Many policy entrepreneurs (and to be honest, not a few professors) play a similar game. They have a solution; now they have to convince the politicians and the public that there is an appropriate problem. Often they fail: despite his best efforts, Robert Bartley of *The Wall Street Journal* never managed to convince many people that monetary chaos looms unless we put America back on the gold standard. Sometimes, however, policy entrepreneurs and the politicians who make alliance with them are spectacularly successful at creating imagined problems to which their favorite policy prescriptions are the answer.

The imaginary problem that galvanized the supply-siders and Ronald Reagan was the danger of Big Government: a government that taxed people too much, then wasted the money on legions of useless bureaucrats and

*This is an excerpt from Paul Krugman, *Peddling Prosperity* (New York: W. W. Norton, 1994). Paul Krugman is professor of economics at Stanford University.

generous welfare handouts to the undeserving poor. Big Government is not, of course, wholly imaginary. Taxes *are* a significant burden on all of us, and there are indeed useless bureaucrats and undeserving welfare recipients. But as a diagnosis of what was wrong with the American economy, it was deeply misleading; and the myth of Big Government both distracted America from coming to grips with its real problems and created new difficulties.

The supply-siders have now retreated to their think tanks, though they still hope to return for revenge. For the time being, Big Government is no longer an effective slogan, and middle-class Americans are angrier at the undeserving rich than the undeserving poor. But the policy entrepreneurs now riding high have convinced many Americans that we have a new kind of trouble in River City: trouble with a capital "C" that stands for "Competitiveness."

The strategic traders have now sold the American public (and for the most part themselves, for only a few policy entrepreneurs are entirely cynical) on the idea that our most crucial economic problem is our struggle with other advanced nations for global markets. The subtitle of Lester Thurow's *Head to Head* is "The Coming Economic Battle Among Japan, Europe, and America"; the jacket entices readers by saying, "The most decisive war of the century is being waged right now . . . and we may have already decided to lose."

Unfortunately, the alleged competitive problem of the United States is as much a fantasy as Reagan's myth of wasteful Big Government. The United States has some real problems in international competition, just as it really has some unproductive bureaucrats and welfare cheats. But in the image it conveys of what's really wrong with the economy, Clinton's rhetoric is as far off as Reagan's.

Economic rhetoric based on the myth of international competition as war has some advantages. It is easier to mobilize voters to support painful policies like tax increases and cuts in popular programs by claiming that the goal is national security—and President Clinton did just that in his highly effective 1993 State of the Union address. But ultimately the rhetoric of competitiveness will be destructive, because it can all too easily lead both to bad policies and to a neglect of the real issues.

The rise of the strategic traders poses two main risks. One is that in their effort to win global markets, they will destroy them instead. The other is that the commitment to a foolish ideology in one area will undermine economic policy across the board.

THE RISK OF TRADE WAR

There are two kinds of trade war: the imaginary ones that protectionists and strategic traders claim we are fighting all the time, and the real ones that happen when they get their way.

The fantasy of the strategic traders is that international trade is by its nature international competition—that countries that trade with each other are in a struggle over who gets the spoils. In reality there is almost nothing to this view: what a country gets depends almost entirely on its own performance, and there is nothing competitive about it. But when countries *believe* that they are in a competitive struggle, or when they become captive to the special interests that benefit from trade conflict, they can fall into what is generally known as a trade war.

A trade war in which countries restrict each other's exports in pursuit of some illusory advantage is not much like a real war. On one hand, nobody gets killed. On the other, unlike real wars, it is almost impossible for anyone to win, since the main losers when a country imposes barriers to trade are not foreign exporters but domestic residents. In effect, a trade war is a conflict in which each country uses most of its ammunition to shoot itself in the foot.

And yet once a trade war is started, it can be very difficult to stop. Each country finds it politically impossible to free up its trade without corresponding "concessions" from other countries, and these may be very hard to negotiate. In other words, once the world has gotten caught up in a wave of tit-for-tat protectionism, it can take decades to undo the damage.

Consider the lessons of the interwar period. A trade war among the advanced countries erupted after the United States passed the infamous Smoot-Hawley tariff in 1929, and intensified as countries made desperate efforts to find ways out of the Great Depression. Yet most people, even including the senators who voted for Smoot-Hawley, soon realized that protectionism had gone too far. The United States began trying to negotiate tariffs down again as early as 1934, and after World War II both the political and the economic environment were very favorable for trade liberalization. Once the global trading system had been shattered, however, it was very hard to put back together; trade among industrial countries didn't regain its 1914 level until 1970.

In the 1990s, the world is ripe for another outbreak of trade war. The key economic ingredients that led to protectionism in the interwar period—slow growth, persistent high unemployment—are back again, especially in Europe. Meanwhile, the political strengths that helped make the freeing up of trade after World War II possible—a strong leading nation and a common purpose—are gone with the relative decline of the United States and the end of the Cold War. It wouldn't take much miscalculation to start a round of tariffs, countertariffs, and mutual recrimination that could repeat the interwar experience of shrinking trade.

Would this be a catastrophe? No, but it would add significantly to our problems. Big, largely self-contained economies like the United States, the European Community, and Japan could take restricted global trade in stride. Even a quite nasty trade war would reduce their real income only a percentage point or two. But smaller countries, more dependent on world markets to help them make up for the small size of their internal markets and their limited resources, would either have to scramble to form commercial alliances with the big players or be left dangerously out in the cold. It would not be surprising if a world of trade conflict among the big advanced countries was a world of political instability, and maybe growing anti-Western feeling, in smaller and poorer countries from Latin America to the former Soviet Republics.

World trade, then, is in an endangered state, in which we could easily stumble into an era of trade conflict that would be at least as hard to get rid of as Ronald Reagan's deficit. Yet it is at this of all moments that strategic traders in the United States think that we need to get tough with other countries in pursuit of "competitiveness."

Imagine the following scenario: Clinton administration officials—ignoring advice from conventional economists—decide that Japan's trade surplus is the root of many of America's economic difficulties, and decide to demand that Japan not only take measures to reduce that surplus but agree to meet specific numerical targets. The Japanese are indignant: they point out, correctly, that it is perfectly reasonable for a country with a very high savings rate to invest a significant fraction of those savings abroad, and that Japan's trade surplus is simply the other side of its capital account deficit. Besides, they say, what are they supposed to do—run huge budget deficits to soak up all that private saving?

The strategic traders in the Clinton administration nonetheless present their demands at an economic summit—and the Japanese reject them. At this point the U.S. government faces a dilemma. To drop the issue would look like weakness; but there is no real policy option other than to close U.S. markets to Japanese goods. And so protectionism it is—a protectionism that is matched by Japanese retaliation and European emulation. Within two years the results of four decades of negotiations to open world markets are reversed.

An unlikely scenario? At the time of writing, much of it had already happened. The Treasury Department is usually a bastion of free trade thinking, but in May 1993 Lawrence Summers, now the Undersecretary of the Treasury for International Affairs, asserted in a speech that "Japan's surplus is the major asymmetry in the global economy" and that this surplus was a "significant drag on global growth"; he followed this assertion with the statement that "The United States will focus less on process and more on results, and results have to be measurable." Everyone knew what he meant: the U.S. Trade Representative had for several weeks been telling reporters that the United States was likely to demand that Japan impose a ceiling on its trade surplus at the next meeting of the Group of Seven industrial countries. Meanwhile, Japanese officials and the Japanese public were furious and defiant in the face of American pressure.

One hopes that by the time this book is published this particular scenario will turn out to have been a premature alarm. As long as the administration is committed to the ideology of strategic trade, however, the risk of trade war will remain high.

So the direct threat from the ascendancy of strategic traders is that their fixation on the supposed problem of competitiveness will set off a trade war. Like the budget deficit created by the supply-siders, a trade war will not destroy the U.S. economy; but also like the budget deficit, it will be very hard to get rid of.

Managed Trade

ROBERT A. LUTZ*

Thank you, Dean Hasler. And good morning to all of you. It's great to be back here at my alma mater. I have a lot of fond memories of Berkeley, starting with the fact that I got a terrific education here from an absolutely brilliant faculty.

I also remember that going to school here—back in those, the earliest days of the Free Speech Movement—was a real lesson in *character-building* for me. You see, I'd already been in the Marine Corps before I started school, and, while in school, I continued as a First Lieutenant in the reserves.

And, since I had a crew cut, an affinity for the military, and wrote letters to the "Daily Californian," I sort of became the resident right-wing speaker at a host of panel discussions around campus. The Free-Speech types didn't want to appear biased, so they put this obviously wacko, lunatic-fringe conservative on their panels just to sort of even things out.

The funny thing, however, is that I was actually a *moderate!* I just *looked* conservative by comparison!

And I must say, it's good to see that things haven't changed much here. I read recently about how you had a student who was coming to class in the nude—"The Naked Guy," I believe he was called? I especially liked it when,

*Robert A. Lutz is president of the Chrysler Corporation. This speech was delivered at the Haas School of Business Faculty–Alumni Colloquium, University of California at Berkeley, on April 24, 1993.

after he got expelled, he said, "My original plan was that I was going to get expelled and then sue for readmittance. *I can learn a lot suing them.*"

Now, I've heard of "independent study," but I think that's a little *ridiculous*—even for Berkeley!

Anyway, it's great to be back here. And I'd like to begin by commending you for choosing a quote-unquote "global focus" for your discussions here at this colloquium today. It's become a cliche, of course, but the business world today truly *is* a global world.

And we in the auto business perhaps know that better than most. Ever since the two oil shocks of the 1970s gave foreign automakers (most notably the Japanese) their first real toehold in this market, we in Detroit have had to struggle with the realities of tough international competition coming at us each and every day right here in our own back yard.

And, though it wasn't always easy, we've learned a lot from that experience.

We've learned, for instance, that over time there's been a certain convergence in consumer tastes around the world. No longer do you have the stereotype of Americans driving nothing but land yachts, Japanese driving nothing but minicars, and Europeans driving spartan econocars. Today, cars like, say, the Honda Accord, the Ford Taurus, or like my company's new Chrysler Concorde, Dodge Intrepid, and Eagle Vision sedans fit in virtually anywhere in the world.

We've also learned that you can run, but you can't hide, when it comes to dealing with international competition. In fact, I daresay that any company today that is still benchmarking just—or even *primarily*—its domestic competitors is probably doomed to failure.

And finally, we've learned that nothing is forever—that, with hard work, even the most seemingly permanent of trends can indeed be turned around. Case in point: In the past 15 months, Chrysler has gained more than two points of total market share in the U.S. And in that same period, the Japanese automakers as a whole have *lost* five-and-a-half points of share. That, I submit, is a *sea change* if there ever was one!

But for all that globalization and international competition has taught us in recent years, we have also learned that global trade has a dark side—a *very* dark side. And that dark side is that not all countries in the world play by the same rules when it comes to international trade.

Oh, sure, everybody pays homage to the GATT, and everybody professes to be "free traders." But, in reality, most everybody in the world—with the notable exception of the United States—practices something that has come to be known as "*managed* trade."

And that's a fact, I know, that the head of President Clinton's Council of Economic Advisors, Berkeley's own Laura D'Andrea Tyson, has herself pointed out many times. The term I believe she likes to use is "aggressive unilateralism." That is, the United States shouldn't be afraid to act *aggressively* and *unilaterally* (if need be) in demanding trade agreements that would, in fact, help *increase* world trade. In other words, in the face of managed trade, we shouldn't be afraid to practice a little managed trade ourselves.

Now, I know that Professor Tyson and others in the Clinton Administration have taken a lot of heat for their views. For example, in the *New York Times* last month, Jagdish Bhagwati of Columbia University said, "This should be the spring of hope, and instead we might get nuclear winter."

Which brings me to the (I hope) rather catchy title of my talk here today: "Managed Trade: Spring of Hope or Nuclear Winter?" In other words: Should managed trade be a part of this country's economic strategy in the context of today's global economy—part of, if you will, our "spring of hope," especially as we strive for some long-overdue economic revitalization?

Or is it, as Professor Bhagwati suggests, a step down a slippery slope leading to a 1930s-style trade war and to a sort of economic nuclear winter?

That's the central question that I'd like to address here today. And by way of illustration, I'd like to use some examples from the auto industry— not just because I know it best, but because the auto industry—the good ol' "smokestack," "sunset" auto industry—is shaping up to be one of *the* prime battlegrounds for global trade issues today. As President Clinton's Trade Representative, Mickey Kantor, put it recently, Detroit is at "the *nerve center* of America's new trade and economic dialogue."

Why? Well, because autos and auto parts have accounted for more than *two-thirds* of America's absolutely staggering $450-*billion*-dollar trade deficit with Japan over the past decade. Obviously, therefore, our *overall* trade deficit cannot come down unless the *auto* deficit is attacked.

Let me tell a story that's been very much in the news lately and which, I think, pretty well symbolizes our whole auto trade with Japan. It's the story of multipurpose vehicles, or "MPVs" for short. An MPV is a vehicle like, say, the Toyota 4-Runner sport utility.

A funny thing happens to a 4-Runner when it's imported into this country. Four U.S. regulators all look it over. The fellow from the Environmental Protection Agency inspects it and declares that it is "a truck," and will therefore only have to meet the emissions standards for U.S. trucks, which are not as strict as those for cars.

Behind him is the man from the National Highway Traffic Safety Administration, who certifies that it is indeed a truck so it won't have to have the same safety devices as a car.

And then comes the inspector from the Department of Transportation, who also agrees that the vehicle is a truck so it won't have to meet the higher fuel economy requirements of a car.

But then comes the fourth inspector. He's from the U.S. Customs Service. He looks at the 4-Runner and says, "Nope, this isn't a truck at all; it's a *car!*" And that means it pays a duty of only 2.5 percent instead of the 25 percent duty on trucks.

Now, what's going on here? Well, back in February of 1989, after intense lobbying by Japanese automakers, the U.S. Treasury Department, in a virtually unprecedented decision, overruled its own Customs Service and reclassified Japanese sport utilities and minivans from trucks to cars. It was, as President Clinton himself put it in a press conference last month, a "$300-million-dollar-a-year freebie to the Japanese for no apparent reason."

Now, maybe it wouldn't have been so bad if the U.S. had gotten some trade concessions *of its own* in return. But we got absolutely *nothing*. Now, I daresay that if a business student here at the Haas School suggested such an obviously win-*lose* deal as a solution to a case study, he'd be joining "The Naked Guy" out on the street!

But that's not the only trade issue related to autos that's been in the news lately. The other one is *dumping*.

As you may know, earlier this year General Motors, Ford, and Chrysler had contemplated filing a dumping charge against Japanese automakers. We had, quite frankly, what we considered to be a *very* strong case. (And it applied, by the way, to *all* major Japanese automakers, across *all* segments of the market—from small cars to luxury cars. And we're talking about cars being dumped for as much as *$5,000* below their prices in Japan. So, this was no inconsequential matter.)

But we backed off—at least for now—in part to give the Clinton Administration a chance to try to solve the problem, and in part, again quite frankly, because of the well-orchestrated negative PR campaign that we were already beginning to experience for even *thinking* about filing a charge.

Now, in concert with that high-priced PR campaign, the Japanese automakers, of course, swore up and down that they were *not* dumping. However, they've nonetheless quietly been raising their prices in recent months (even *before* the yen started to rise)—which might, I think, lead a cynic to believe that just maybe they'd rather pocket the money themselves than have the U.S. government get it in added tariffs!

Meanwhile, amid all the PR and all of the mud-slinging, a couple of simple things seemed to have gotten lost: One is that dumping is *against the law*—against both U.S. *and* international trade law. And Japan certainly knows that as well as anybody, given that they just recently imposed anti-dumping duties of *their own*—on manganese coming in from China!

The other thing that seems to have gotten lost is that "managed trade" is really *already* being practiced here in the United States—only it's all too often the *Japanese*, and not us, who are managing it!

Now, at this point, I know that perhaps some of you might be inclined to say, "Hey, why don't you guys in Detroit quit whining, and just shut up and compete?"

Well, we *are* competing. Earlier, I mentioned the market share that we at Chrysler have won back here in the U.S. We've also, by the way, been doing quite well in Europe. From a virtual standstill, we've sold more than 200,000 vehicles in Europe in the last four years. And so far *this* year, our European sales are *up* 30 percent, while the market as a whole is *down* 17 percent.

But the one place where we continue to have very little success at all is—you guessed it—*Japan.*

And it's not just us—*no* foreign automakers really have had any success to speak of in Japan. In fact, total import penetration in the Japanese auto market was less than *three* percent last year. By contrast, the Japanese have routinely taken up to *ten times* that amount of the U.S. market (and here in California, of course, it's been more like *15* times).

Now, why is that? Well, let me cite the case of Chrysler's new Jeep Grand Cherokee sport utility (which, by the way, competes head to head with the Toyota 4-Runner). The Grand Cherokee is, by any measure, a world-class vehicle. It won Motor Trend's "Truck of the Year" award last year. And it's completely sold out both here in the United States and in Europe.

Yet we have a tough time selling Grand Cherokees *in Japan.* And no wonder, given that they cost over $15,000 *more* in Japan than they do here!

That's because the Japanese won't accept our certifications, because everything has to be inspected, and mostly because of the maze of red tape and gargantuan distribution costs associated with Japan's notoriously closed distribution system.

And "closed" it is. In fact, until just recently, Japanese automakers prevented their dealers in Japan from selling any imported cars at all!

Now, if we did this in the U.S., of course, we'd be thrown in jail for violating antitrust laws. But in Japan, it's been standard practice. And, as a result, while foreign cars are sold today at more than *90* percent of all dealerships in the United States, foreign cars are sold at just *seven* percent of all dealerships in Japan!

But, of course, it's not just cars that have been kept out of Japan. The list of products is, in my view, embarrassingly long. And, of course, as the folks down in Silicon Valley know all too well, that list includes *computer chips.*

Now, I understand that trade tensions eased a bit out here recently when it was announced that, in the fourth quarter, U.S. and other foreign semi-conductor makers had finally—*finally*—achieved the target of 20 percent of the Japanese chip market. But I think it's worth keeping in mind *how* our chip makers actually achieved that goal.

The process began way back in 1985, when the Reagan Administration (of all people!) accepted an anti-dumping case and a "Super 301" unfair trade case brought against the Japanese. That "chip shot," as it was called, then eventually led to negotiations, which, in turn, produced the 20-percent import target. (And I understand, by the way, that that 20-percent figure is still less than *half* the market share that U.S. chip makers enjoy *elsewhere* in the world. And it's also almost identical to the share of the *U.S.* chip market that *Japanese* companies enjoy!)

Anyway, the upshot is that in the case of computer chips the U.S. followed a policy of, yes, *managed trade.* In fact, it was one that definitely contained some Laura Tyson-style "aggressive unilateralism." And, lo and behold, it's *working*!

Now, I know that Professor Tyson along with others in the Administration, such as Mickey Kantor, have been called "trade agnostics" for their pragmatic, results-oriented approach to global trade. And I'm sure those who say that often mean it in a derogatory sense—that Tyson and Kantor and others have somehow lost their ideological souls.

But I, for one, think there's a big difference between being a trade *atheist* (that is, somebody who *has* lost his soul and given up on free trade altogether) and a trade *agnostic.* A trade agnostic, it seems to me, is someone who believes that real free trade could indeed exist in the world someday—but who in the meantime speaks softly and carries a big stick!

By that definition, the *Europeans,* to name just one example, are certainly trade agnostics. Last year—as part of the "EC '92" negotiations—the European Community told Japanese automakers that they can have no more than *16 percent* of the European auto market through the end of this century. (That compares, despite their recent losses, to the *24*-percent share of the market that the Japanese have in the *U.S.* today.)

Now, I know that Professor Tyson herself might even say that an industry like autos is too mature, and too "low-tech," to qualify for the benefits of managed trade here in this country.

But, for starters, we're hardly low-tech. You may not know this, but the auto industry buys *20 percent*—that's *one in five*—of all the semiconductors sold in this country. In fact, a car today with an air bag, ABS brakes, and traction control has the computing power of the on-board guidance system of the Apollo moonshot!

(And, by the way, I think that Silicon Valley should be more than a little dismayed by reports recently that while U.S. chip makers supply *60* percent of the chips that go into luxury cars worldwide—the kind of cars most likely *to have* traction control and that other high-tech stuff—their market share of the Japanese luxury brands Lexus and Infiniti is just *seven* percent!)

And as far as being a so-called "mature" industry goes—yes, the auto industry is guilty of being mature. But the fact is, every industry in this country *aspires* to be mature one day. We *all* want to perpetuate ourselves. But think about this: If we allow *today's* high-employment, high-value-added, mature industries to become victims of *somebody else's* managed-trade policies, than what does that bode for the mature industries of *tomorrow?*

Going back to Europe, the Europeans have basically said that their key, strategic industries, including autos, and the jobs that they represent are *important* to them. Now, maybe in the case of Airbus and agricultural subsidies, they've gone overboard a little bit! But by and large, they have, in my opinion, found a much better trade-off than we have between the so-called "rights of the consumer" and *also*-very-legitimate rights of those very same citizens to be gainfully employed.

Which makes sense. After all, if you think about it, the most useless consumer of all is one *without a job!*

For some reason, we haven't seemed quite ready to grasp that reality here in this country. Although in this so-called "jobless recovery" of ours, and with all of the so-called "hollowing-out" of American industry that's taken place over the last decade or so (including the layoffs at IBM and elsewhere in high tech), I think maybe we're *beginning* to understand.

And I also think that we're finally beginning to understand that our trade policies (or lack thereof) have definitely played a *key role* in that hollowing-out and in that joblessness.

So, to get back to my central question—"Managed Trade: Spring of Hope or Nuclear Winter?"—I think, in truth, that we are actually experiencing a bit of "nuclear winter" *right now!* (Or maybe you might call it *"neutron* winter"—the buildings are still standing, it's just the *jobs* that are gone!)

I also think that if we want to get this economy moving strongly forward again, and *keep* it moving forward as a global leader into the 21st century, then there's no doubt that a more pragmatic—indeed, one might say a more *realistic*—trade policy needs to be adopted. *That,* in my opinion, is our "spring of hope."

And if that sounds like "trade agnosticism," then so be it. But in my book, it makes a whole lot more sense to be an agnostic on this subject than a so-called "true believer" who keeps waiting for his savior . . . but in the meantime winds up getting crucified *himself!*

And on that note, I'd like to thank you for letting this "prodigal-son-of-Berkeley-turned-trade-agnostic" return to his alma mater to offer his I-hope-not-*too*-blasphemous opinions.

If nothing else, it's nice knowing, all these years later, that I'm probably no longer the resident conservative here on campus!

Thank you very much.

U.S. Trade Deficits and International Competitiveness

ROBERT T. PARRY*

T hank you. It's a pleasure to be here. Today I'd like to talk about our trade deficit and what it implies about our ability to compete globally. We've had this trade deficit for over a decade. Some people, and a number of policymakers, see this as a symptom that we've lost our edge in international competition. Here's their diagnosis of the problem: Foreign competitors are able to take markets away from U.S. producers because they have some important advantages. In particular, they have lower wages, superior technology, and "unfair" trade practices.

What's their prescription to fix the problem and return U.S. industries to competitive health? They'd like to see the government try to manage international competition by taking a more protectionist stance and targeting certain industries for special support.

My own view is that this analysis is off the mark. I do *not* think the trade deficit is due to lower wages, superior technology, and "unfair" trade practices abroad. On the contrary, I think we can find the sources of the trade deficit in certain macroeconomic fundamentals—namely, our own government budget deficit and our investment and saving patterns. Moreover, I don't think the trade deficit is necessarily the best way to judge our com-

*Robert T. Parry is president of the Federal Reserve Bank of San Francisco. This speech was delivered to the National Association of Business Economists in Chicago, Illinois, on September 20, 1993.

188

petitiveness. There are more important factors to consider. In particular, I would point to price competitiveness and productivity.

Let me begin by looking at just how bad the trade deficit is. First, I think it's a mistake to focus too much on the most recent numbers, which haven't been too good. The reason it's a mistake is that the source of the problem is more cyclical than it is structural. The U.S. has been in recovery for a while now. But many of our industrial trading partners are still in recession. So the recent bulge in our trade deficit is largely due to the fact that, as we continue to grow and import more, the weakness abroad is hurting our exports.

Now let me look at the longer view. Although the trade deficit has persisted for over a decade, the situation is much better now than it was in the mid-1980s. The merchandise trade deficit fell from a peak of $160 billion in 1987 to $96 billion in 1992. Relative to GDP, it declined from 3.5 percent to 1.6 percent. The current account deficit, which includes trade in services, improved even more dramatically. It dropped from a deficit of $167 billion in 1987 to $62 billion in 1992—or from 3.5 percent of GDP to 1 percent of GDP.

Why the turnaround? Because over the past six years, U.S. exports have surged. From 1986 through 1992 the total value of U.S. merchandise exports almost doubled, growing more than 12 percent per year. In volume terms, exports grew almost as fast, averaging more than 10 percent per year. A major source of strength in this export growth has been manufactures. And it's notable that this sector has continued to show strength even during the worldwide economic slowdown of the past few years. So the big picture on the trade deficit is that the situation is better than it was in the mid-1980s, because U.S. exports have surged since then.

Now let me look at the problem of "unfair trade practices." By this I mean such things as government support of selected industries through export subsidies and trade protection. The evidence is clear that virtually all countries, including the U.S., impose at least some restrictions on imports and provide government support for exports. Still, there's *no* evidence that the U.S. trade deficits of the 1980s were caused by greater foreign trade barriers or other unfair trade practices. First of all, between 1981 and 1987, when the deficit was at its peak, the deterioration in our trade position was *pervasive*. It spread uniformly and proportionately across capital goods, automotive products, and consumer goods. And the deterioration was roughly in proportion to each of our major trading partner's share of U.S. import and exports in 1981. If unfair foreign trade practices had caused the pervasive decline in the early 1980s, they would have had to change uniformly and suddenly around 1981, an unlikely conspiracy.

Of all the U.S. trading partners, Japan continues to be singled out for having the most unfair trading practices. But it's doubtful that such policies have been a major cause of U.S. trade deficits. First of all, the Japanese market has become somewhat more *open*—not more closed—over the past decade. Second, Japan's share of changes in the total U.S. non-oil merchandise trade deficit have been proportional to its U.S. trade share. For example, in 1981, about 9 percent of our exports went to Japan, and about 20 percent of our imports came from Japan. That left us with a bilateral deficit of $16 billion. If the same shares prevailed in 1992, we would have had a bilateral deficit of $57 billion—which is in fact a little larger than the actual deficit of $51 billion. So I think there's not much evidence to say that restrictive trade practices have been the driving force behind changes in the U.S. trade deficit.

Of course, the doors to Japanese and other foreign markets aren't exactly wide open to U.S. exporters. But even if existing foreign restrictions on U.S. exports were completely removed, most estimates suggest we'd reduce our trade deficit by only modest amounts.

Now let me look at our international competitiveness in terms of our production costs and productivity. Is there any evidence that U.S. price competitiveness declined during the 1980s? If we make the comparison in dollar terms, then the answer is: "Yes, price competitiveness *did* decline." Between 1980 and 1985 unit labor costs in dollars rose at an annual rate of 3.1 percent in the U.S., while unit labor costs fell in 10 of 11 other industrial countries.

But that information doesn't give us a complete picture. If we make the comparison in national currency terms, then unit labor costs actually *rose* in most of those other countries. Therefore, it was the appreciation of the dollar in the early 1980s, not underlying cost increases, that primarily caused U.S. manufacturers to lose price competitiveness to foreign producers during this period.

The fall of the dollar since the mid-1980s has made foreign unit labor costs measured in dollars now substantially higher than they were in 1980. Between the 1985 peak in the dollar and 1992, U.S. unit labor costs rose at only 1 percent per year, while costs in Japan, France, Germany, Korea, and Taiwan, for example, all rose at roughly 10 percent annually over the period 1985–1992. Therefore, most of the apparent improvement in U.S. international competitiveness is due to changes in the value of the dollar. Furthermore, manufacturing in the U.S. now appears to have a significant cost advantage over manufacturing in other countries.

What about productivity? The U.S. had relatively *strong* productivity growth during the 1980s. Between 1980 and 1985, manufacturers' output per worker grew 3.3 percent annually in the U.S., compared to 4.0 percent in Japan, 2.3 percent in France, and 2.1 percent in Germany. Since the mid-1980s U.S. productivity has continued to keep pace and even exceed that in much of the rest of the world. From 1985 to 1992 U.S. manufacturing output per worker grew at 2.9 percent per year, compared to 2.3 percent in Japan, 0.8 percent in Germany, and 2.8 percent in France.

Now that we can't blame the trade deficit on our competitors' lower labor costs, higher productivity, or unfair trade practices, where do we look for the source of it? The answer, I think, is in macroeconomic fundamentals. By definition, a country's trade balance is the mirror image of its pattern of saving and investment. So, for example, a country with more investment opportunities than its domestic saving can handle will borrow from abroad and run a trade deficit. This is true even if its costs are relatively low, its home markets are protected, and its exports are subsidized. The converse also holds true: A country with high saving relative to investment will run trade *surpluses*—even if its markets are open and its products are regarded as "noncompetitive."

In the case of the U.S., the emergence and persistence of large trade deficits since the early 1980s can be attributed largely to changes in the nation's saving-investment balance. Over the 1960s and 1970s, the U.S. (gross) national saving rate roughly equaled the investment rate and remained constant at about 20 percent of GNP. As a result the current account remained approximately in balance. But in the early 1980s, the national saving rate fell, largely because of bigger government budget deficits. The resulting net saving deficit led to higher real interest rates, the appreciation of the dollar, and the associated current account deficits that emerged in the early 1980s. In the second half of the 1980s the budget deficit turned around somewhat, interest rates and the dollar fell, and the current account deficit began to narrow.

So it's primarily *macroeconomic developments* that explain the worsening of the U.S. trade balance in the early 1980s followed by its improvement later in the decade. To keep the trend of improvement going in the long run, we'll need further macroeconomic policy adjustments. Ideally, we'd accomplish this through either a fiscal contraction or an increase in private saving. Less ideally, we could accomplish it through a reduction in domestic investment. The current plans for reduced federal budget deficits are in the right direction.

In conclusion, I think the U.S. is in reasonably good competitive shape. U.S. exports have boomed and the trade deficit is lower than it was in the mid-1980s. More important, measures of labor costs and productivity, particularly in manufacturing, indicate resurgent U.S. price competitiveness. U.S. productivity growth in the 1980s has been comparable with and, in some cases better than, other industrial countries abroad. The continued existence of U.S. trade deficits reflects an imbalance of national saving below investment, not any fundamental decline in U.S. international competitiveness.

Of course, when you talk about competition, you're always talking about winners and losers. And there's no question that some industries are going to continue to face difficult times from foreign competitors. But the real winners will be consumers for whom foreign competition means better quality U.S. products. The experience of the U.S. automobile industry is a case in point. Moreover, in a dynamic competitive world economy, with new products, technologies, and production processes continually becoming available, there will always be some firms on the decline as others are on the rise. The appropriate policy response to an industry that's losing ground to foreign competition is not to erect barriers to imports, but rather to facilitate the redirection of workers who lose jobs to more productive employment opportunities elsewhere. If the protectionist route is followed, newer, more efficient industries will have less scope to expand, and overall output and economic welfare will suffer.

And this brings me back to the main question of this conference: U.S. prosperity in a competitive world. The real issue of our long-term prosperity, of maintaining and improving American living standards, doesn't depend on how stiff the competition is abroad. It depends primarily on our *own* productivity growth and our ability to maintain a stable economic environment. The Federal Reserve has a role in this, of course. And that is to conduct a low-inflation monetary policy. But that's not enough. This country also must grapple with the hard issues of devising the means to boost productivity—

☐ with policies that foster greater private capital formation,

☐ with policies that increase investment in infrastructure,

☐ with policies that expand research and development expenditures,

☐ with policies that improve the quality of education,

☐ and with policies that stimulate entrepreneurial activity.

To sum this all up: Our prosperity doesn't depend on distorting markets with industrial policies and protectionist barriers; instead it depends on improving our productivity and letting markets work to bring out the best in our natural and human resources.

Thank you.

QUESTIONS FOR ANALYSIS

1. Professor Krugman seems to fear that a trade war may break out between the United States and Japan. Why?

2. If a trade war were to break out, would it matter? Why or why not?

3. If the United States has a comparative advantage in the production of pharmaceuticals and if Japan has a comparative advantage in the production of autos, what are the advantages in the U.S.'s specialization in pharmaceuticals and Japan's specialization in autos?

4. If the United States has a comparative advantage in the production of pharmaceuticals, can we be sure that the United States will be an exporter of pharmaceuticals? Why or why not?

5. Mr. Lutz states that: "Last year . . . the European Community told Japanese automakers that they can have no more than *16 percent* of the European auto market through the end of this century." What groups gain from this policy, and why? What groups lose from this policy, and why?

6. Mr. Lutz goes on to say that "the Europeans have basically said that their key, strategic industries, including autos, and the jobs that they represent are *important* to them . . . [B]y and large, they have, in my opinion, found a much better trade-off than we have between the so-called 'rights of the consumer' and *also*-very-legitimate rights of those very same citizens to be gainfully employed." Why does Mr. Lutz believe such a tradeoff exists? Do you agree? Why or why not?

7. According to Mr. Lutz, "earlier this year General Motors, Ford, and Chrysler had contemplated filing a dumping charge against Japanese automakers . . . (And we're talking about cars being dumped for as much as $5,000 below their prices in Japan. So, this was no inconsequential matter.)" What is wrong with Japanese automakers selling their cars in the United States for $5,000 less than in Japan?

8. Mr. Parry does "*not* think that the trade deficit is due to lower wages, superior technology, and 'unfair' trade practices abroad. On the contrary, [he thinks] we can find the sources of the trade deficit in certain macroeconomic fundamentals—namely, our own government budget deficit and our investment and saving patterns." What has the government budget deficit got to do with our trade deficit? Is it true that our investment and saving patterns are related to our trade deficit? If so, explain in detail what the relationships are.

9. According to Mr. Parry, "I don't think the trade deficit is necessarily the best way to judge our competitiveness. There are more important factors to consider. In particular, I would point to price competitiveness and productivity." Why are these factors important in this regard?

10. Mr. Parry concludes that: "Our prosperity doesn't depend on distorting markets with industrial policies and protectionist barriers; instead it depends on improving our productivity and letting markets work to bring out the best in our natural and human resources." Do you agree? Why or why not?

11. Mr. Parry points out that productivity in manufacturing grew more rapidly during 1985–92 in the United States than in Japan, Germany, or France. Does this mean that productivity in the entire economy grew faster in the United States than in these other countries? What are the problems in measuring productivity in industries producing services? Will the rate of productivity growth be increased by policies that (a) increase private capital formation, (b) expand research and development expenditures, (c) improve the quality of education?

12. What can the federal government do to (a) increase private capital formation, (b) expand research and development, (c) improve the quality of education?

PART TEN

ECONOMIC

REFORM IN

EASTERN

EUROPE

One of the most significant developments of recent years has been the movement of the Eastern European countries away from central planning and toward capitalism. This movement is by no means easy, and some countries have had much more success than others in making the transition. In the first article, Boris Yeltsin, President of the Russian Federation, describes the economic policy of Russia, with particular attention to his economic goals and the problems faced by the Russian people. In the second article, Václav Klaus, prime minister of the Czech Republic, discusses the interplay of political and economic factors in the transformation process. Needless to say, their views, which differ considerably, are controversial.

The Economic Policy of Russia

BORIS YELTSIN*

Distinguished Chairman of the Federation Council and State Duma! Distinguished members of the Federation Council! Distinguished deputies to the State Duma! I have a special feeling ascending to this rostrum. Today's statement is a truly extraordinary event in my life and political career. It is for the first time that the new Russian parliament receives a presidential address. Russia begins to develop a new approach to policy planning.

Momentous efforts were attached to produce this address. The problem was that I wanted to squeeze too much into this message, and even more has to be accomplished. Therefore, it is essential to see that our resources, political will, intellectual potential and tremendous will of the people to live better are not pulverized but be focused on key areas and we may produce tangible results by concerted effort.

This is why my address contains an outline of the current situation and some ideas for the future you suggested during the election campaign and afterwards. . .

Most people are permanently anxious over their future, the future of their children and retired parents. In the meanwhile, federal and local authorities prefer to give a blind eye to the rapid social stratification. We have

*Boris Yeltsin is President of the Russian Federation. This speech was delivered to the Federal Assembly in Moscow, Russia, on February 24, 1994.

to responsibly admit that we underestimate all threats that stratification harbours.

I am not appealing to come back to former notorious egalitarian practices, when all people were supposed to be equally poor and better off people ripped off. However, this delicate and painful issue shall not be left until it solves by itself.

We are bitterly learning that the state-ruled self-consuming economy, in which ten people are busy with the work that can be reasonably done by one person, has no future.

We don't have a normal market economy so far. On the other hand, swindlers and rippers are feeling nice and easy. Honest and industrious people, who don't fear to be self-employed have enormous difficulties in getting on.

My heart is breaking to say this, but it is true. We have greater freedom in this country, yes. But this is not enough. Our strategic goal is to develop justice, security and confidence in Russia. . .

We need a general programme of state reforms in the Russian Federation. Here are its goals:

One. The state authorities should not work for themselves, but rather for Russia's interests and those of its citizens, which have been precisely revealed and formulated. This implies a transition from impulse responses to a strategy based on well-thought-out anticipatory steps.

Two. Power must be efficient. This implies a striving and ability to finish off what has been started and assess in the strictest possible manner the potential costs of decisions, which are to be taken.

Legal reform plays an important role here. A strong third estate doesn't weaken the other estates: on the contrary, it merely strengthens them. I accord special significance to the Constitutional Court, which must interpret the Constitution objectively.

Local self-government must be developed: it must be given a legal base. Perhaps we should therefore   contemplate together the election dates. One must accord serious consideration to army reforms. The state border regime and many other issues must be streamlined.

Three. We must bring an end to the bureaucracy's boundless nature, when any sensible decisions and initiatives are strangled by the deathly embrace of the bureaucracy. This goal can be achieved by well-known methods—a precise regulation of functions and responsibilities. Unfortunately, we lack this at present.

Four. Power must become open and understandable to the people. That means that we must develop a dialogue, contribute to the formation of a civic society. Power should not be screened off from the mass media, but rather aid and abet the latter and bring about the denationalisation of the press. . .

We have seen from our own experience that without a strong, effective state we will not overcome the economic crisis, create a true market economy, make the economic situation predictable or create conditions for economic growth.

I know that the people in Russia and abroad became worried over the economic policy of Russia after the December elections and reshuffles in the Government.

I want to dispel these worries. As long as I remain the President of Russia, I will protect and advocate the policy of economic reforms. In 1994 the continuation of the economic reforms will be a priority of Russia's internal policy.

In the past few years we have developed several major elements of market relations, such as economic freedom, the right of ownership, and working markets of goods and services. But it is too early yet to say that the Russian economy lives by market laws. What we have is a combination of new, still weak market mechanisms and old command bureaucratic levers.

The administrative distribution system has not disappeared without a trace; it changed. The bureaucrat who once drafted plans and distributed funds, has learned the doings of the market and distributes (and sometimes sells) central quotas and licenses. Lobby trends are developing, and the reform of the economic mechanism is proceeding very unstably.

We know the result: the crisis does not abate, the production slump slows, but continues, and viable enterprises stop production. Inflation is wearing out the country. Social tensions remain very high.

The greatest mistake we can make today is to offer society a false alternative: either the past state-directive economy, or the so-called pure market, absolutely independent of the state. Both alternatives would be fatal for Russia and its economy.

The task is to find a reasonable combination of the speed of reforms and their real social costs, use the powerful, but so far idling, reserves of the reforms, and find optimum ways of state participation in economic processes.

The past two years showed that not only the reforms entail social outlays. We suffer even greater damage from the delays in long-overdue changes in the economic mechanism.

It is time to establish effective state regulation compatible with market mechanisms. This is a priority task of the current stage of the reforms.

The state should be the master of the state economic sector. Otherwise we will not overcome chaos and stop the squandering of the state sector by some economic managers.

We must continue to liberalise exports, and at the same time strengthen control over the export of strategic raw materials and energy carriers.

The government must strengthen hard currency control. It is vital to establish severe sanctions against violators who illegally keep hard currency abroad. . .

The year 1994 must see the beginning of a restructuring of the Russian economy. Russia must produce only those goods which are needed by the public, state, and the world market. We must stop producing goods not needed by anyone.

This is a very hard and expensive task to handle. It cannot be solved in a short time or by bans. However, this does not mean that we should again avoid doing this. Has the government not yet become convinced that without a restructuring policy we will have structural degradation?

Structural degradation is already here. We are gradually losing modern technological infrastructure and major sectors, hightech products, in particular. We are beginning to lag behind not only of the best world achievements but also of ourselves.

The principle of "let survive those who can survive" is disastrous. In today's Russia the survivors are not those who make the best quality goods. Or, at least, not only they alone. The survivors are people with the maximum of benefits and privileges, those who are patronised by authorities and who know how to squeeze money from the government.

If this trend goes on, Russia may become a market economy but this will be a primitive and inefficient economy.

The government should have long determined its structural priorities and act accordingly.

What is it that interferes with our choice of strategic sectors, internationally competitive and socially important for Russia? These sectors, experts say, do not exceed 10 percent of Russian production. These sectors should have normal state support in the next few years. This support to other sectors should be slashed down and targeted.

It is time we decide what products are needed by the state and how much of them. Here I mean, among other things, the defence contract.

The managers of major plants have begged me more than once to ask the government to tell them whether to produce one or another article or not. Yes or no.

"Yes" means that the government should honour its financial commitments. "No" means the government should not stand in the way of these plants switching to civilian products.

A major reserve of the reform is demonopolisation of Russian production. We will not have a normal economy as long as one producer dictates its terms to others only because it is the monopolist in its field.

Monopolism in Russia developed over decades. In fact, it was an official policy which devoured tremendous funds and resources. Demonopolisation will also require a major effort and time. We should begin with demonopolisation in an effective way.

Investment policy is another major resource of the reform. To the accompaniment of the talk about an investment crisis and the state lacking money to support producers, tremendous funds are being pumped into favourite sectors and producers. However, investment activity is still at a very low point.

The sole way to improve things here is to resort to a precise investment policy. The role of investment policy grows immensely now that the crisis and inflation are ravaging and the state's financial capability is at its minimum.

The government should have long introduced and monitored a uniform procedure of state support appropriation.

There is no end to the talk about the investment process being incompatible with inflation. This verbiage leaves us a precious little time to form the necessary institutions and structures and develop legislation here.

The practical effort to make things here attractive to foreign investors is very modest. I hear reproaches on this score whenever I talk with foreign businessmen in America, Britain, Japan or China.

It is obvious that until domestic entrepreneurs invest their money in the Russian economy our foreign partners will abstain from major investments in this country. The Russian state must steadily uphold the interests of Russian companies at home and internationally.

We have other reserves too. Upon the end of the voucher stage of privatisation we should resolutely steer towards new objectives. Privatisation should be attractive to investors, domestic and foreign alike. This year privatisation should be more fruitful for the economy than it was until now.

Nineteen ninety-four must become the year of practical state support for the producer. . . .

Interplay of Political and Economic Reform Measures

VÁCLAV KLAUS*

The worldwide breakdown of communism at the end of the eighties gives us a unique (we may say an epochal) opportunity to get rid of the irrationalities and injustices of the old, discredited communist regime and to build on its ruins a standard system of political pluralism and democracy and of unconstrained market economy. The country I represent here tonight, the Czech Republic, is in this respect no exception. If there is anything particular about my country, anything I should—with unhidden pride and satisfaction—stress here, it is its relatively very fast progress in both political and economic components of the transformation process. I believe that the Czech Republic has already crossed the Rubicon dividing the old and the new regime. It is an important achievement; we may become the proof that the transformation from communism to a free society can be realized.

The topic of my concern as well as curiosity is to search for the reasons of visible and irrefutable differences in the speed as well as in the nature of the transformation process we observe in various postcommunist countries these days. I will draw on my experience to outline some of the underlying principles of an optimal reform strategy for all countries that may find themselves facing a similar challenge as my country.

*Václav Klaus is prime minister of the Czech Republic. He delivered this speech at the Heritage Foundation in Washington, D.C., on October 15, 1993.

Even without a detailed and profound analysis, it is apparent that there are postcommunist countries with very modest success; countries which have fallen into what I call the "reform trap"; countries which have fallen into the vicious circle of incomplete and incorrect reform measures, of increasing inflation and unemployment, of public budget deficits and foreign indebtedness, of accelerating political troubles, of myopic policies which generate even worse outcomes, of chaos and anarchy, etc. We know that such a process usually ends in a deep political-economic crisis and in the further undermining of chances for success.

There are, however, countries which have succeeded in avoiding the fall into the reform trap; countries that were able to initiate *a virtuous circle* based on a mixture of reasonable and therefore effective reform measures. Such a circle brings about positive economic results, political stability, continuation of reforms, etc.

The huge differences we witness are, in my opinion, the result of a specific interplay of political and economic factors in the transformation process. These factors support and complement each other. For me, the central role of such an interplay between economic policies and the political environment is self-evident, but it is often forgotten or at least not fully appreciated.

The systemic transformation is not an exercise in applied economics or in applied political science; it is a process which involves human beings, which affects their day-to-day life, which creates new groups of gainers and losers, which changes the relative political and economic strength and standing of different socio-economic groups and which, therefore, destroys the original political, social, and economic equilibrium. The communist system was characterized by its own, peculiar, relatively stable equilibrium. Whether the new equilibrium and especially the path from one equilibrium to another becomes stable or unstable depends upon the aforementioned interplay.

What are the lessons I can draw from our experience?

1) To be successful, the political leaders must formulate and sell to the citizens of the country a positive vision of a future society.

The first task is its formulation. The vision must be positive (not just a negative one); it must be straightforward (not fuzzy); it must motivate; it must speak to the hearts of the men and women who spent most of their lives in the spiritually empty communist regime. It requires clear words— biblical yes, yes, no, no; it must be stated in an ideal form (which needs "extreme" terms, because the compromises belong to reality, not to images or visions); it must explicitly reject all forms of "third ways," which are based on incompatible combinations of different worlds.

The communist regime demonstrated, and we have fully understood, that human nature does not want "brave new worlds" (to use Aldous Huxley's apt term) and that to construct a free and functioning societal system on dreams, on moral imperatives, or on somebody else's preferences is absolutely impossible. We accept Adam Smith's teaching. His vision of a free, democratic, and efficient civic society where the citizen, and not an enlightened monarch or an elitist intellectual is the king, is our vision. Because of that, to fulfill this first task—to formulate a vision—is not difficult. It requires just "to know" and to follow proven, conservative principles.

The second task, to sell the vision, is much more complicated. It requires to address the people, to argue, to explain, to defend; it requires permanent campaigning. It requires more than a good communications system, more than sophisticated information technology, more than free and independent mass media. It requires the formation of standard political parties, because without them the politicians have no real power base and there is no mechanism to democratically create politicians, ideologies, and visions. Most postcommunist countries started the transformation without established political parties (and without positive visions as well) and were, therefore, unable to establish a basic, sufficiently strong pro-reform consensus and to start introducing necessary reform steps.

The political and social cohesion of a country cannot be cultivated without a permanent interaction of political parties. This is something the citizens (and politicians) in post-communist countries were not accustomed to. To overcome their distrust of political parties is not easy, but it must be done as soon as possible.

2) The necessary set of reform steps must include both changes of institutions and changes of behavioral and regulatory rules, i.e., changes of the rules of a game.

Without profound institutional changes we cannot establish new agents in the game: citizens, political parties, and parliaments in the political sphere; consumers and suppliers of labor, firms, independent central banks, and "small" and constitutionally constrained governments in the economic sphere (to name the most important ones). Those changes create a totally new institutional (or organizational) structure of the whole society.

Rules are changed by new, spontaneously created habits and customs as well as by new legislation and by subsequent policies. Their substance is on the one hand to deregulate and liberalize, and on the other to define principal constraints and limits of the decision-making spaces of participating agents. That is the only way to unlock markets, to unleash private initiative, to eliminate excessive state interference, to let the newly formed agents behave in a rational way.

Institutional changes take time. Changes of rules, however, can and must be done very fast. Much of the disagreement about the speed of transformation (shock therapy or gradualism) can be dispelled if a proper distinction is made between the speed of those two conceptually different transformation tasks.

3) Such a fundamental change of an entire society cannot be dictated by *a priori,* preplanned, or prearranged procedures. Reform blueprints must be loose, unpretentious, and flexible. The dreams of social engineers of all ideological colors to organize or to mastermind the whole process of a systemic transformation in a rigid way are false, misleading, and dangerous. It must be accepted—as an important transformation theorem—that it is impossible to centrally plan the origin and rise of a free society and of a market economy.

The reformers must accept that this process involves not just them but millions of human beings with their own dreams, preferences, and priorities. The role of politicians in it must be, therefore, rather limited. They can guide and inspire, introduce necessary legislative amendments, implement appropriate policies; they should not, however, try to dictate, command, order. Democracy is indispensable and attempts to ignore it in the name of easier and faster reforms are futile and ineffective.

4) The reforms must be bold, courageous, determined, and therefore, painful, because

□ economic activities based on subsidized prices, on artificially created (and now non-existent) demands, and on sheltered markets must cease to exist;

□ once-and-for-all price jumps after price deregulation are unavoidable;

□ drastic devaluation, inevitable to introduce before liberalization of foreign trade, shifts the exchange rate very far below the purchasing power parity;

□ income and property disparities grow to an unprecedented level, etc.

These changes and their impacts must be preannounced, preexplained, vigorously defended, and "survived." The costs the people have to bear must be widely shared, otherwise the fragile political support is lost. Telling the truth, not promising things which cannot be realized, and guarding credibility of reform programs and of politicians who realize them are absolute imperatives.

Once-and-for-all-changes constitute necessary byproducts of any kind of a systemic transformation; galloping inflations or hyperinflations, repeated devaluations, prolonged GDP declines, state budget deficits, and growing foreign indebtedness are, however, avoidable by a positive interplay of political and economic reforms and by introduction and implementation of rational macroeconomic policies, based on conservative foundations. Monetarism, not Keynesianism; fixed-rules, not fine-tuning; balanced budgets, not fiscal activism; self-reliance, not dependence on foreign mercenaries: these are the inspiring words for all of us who want to accomplish the historic transformation, for all of us who want to create a free, democratic, and efficient society.

QUESTIONS FOR ANALYSIS

1. In what respects can a free-market economy be expected to out-perform a centrally planned economy?

2. What are the limitations of a free-market economy?

3. According to President Yeltsin, "The greatest mistake we can make today is to offer society a false alternative: either the past state-directive economy, or the so-called pure market, absolutely independent of the state. Both alternatives would be fatal for Russia and its economy." What other alternatives exist?

4. In President Yeltsin's view, "The principle of 'let survive those who can survive' is disastrous. In today's Russia the survivors are not those who make the best quality goods. Or, at least, not only they alone. The survivors are people with the maximum of benefits and privileges, those who are patronised by authorities and who know how to squeeze money from the government." Does this mean that Adam Smith's "invisible hand" really does not work, at least in Russia? Why or why not?

5. President Yeltsin states that: "We will not have a normal economy as long as one producer dictates its terms to others only because it is the monopolist in its field. . . . We should begin with demonopolisation in an effective way." What measures might be taken to accomplish this?

6. Prime Minister Klaus argues that "Institutional changes take time. Changes of rules, however, can and must be done very fast. Much of the disagreement about the speed of transformation (shock therapy or gradualism) can be dispelled if a proper distinction is made between the speed of those two conceptually different transformation tasks." What does he mean by rules? What does he mean by institutions? Why can the former be changed more rapidly than the latter?

7. In Prime Minister Klaus's view, "Monetarism, not Keynesianism; fixed-rules, not fine-tuning; balanced budgets, not fiscal activism; self-reliance, not dependence on foreign mercenaries: these are the inspiring words for all of us who want to accomplish the historic transformation. . . . " Do you think that this view is shared by most people in the United States? Do you agree with him? Why or why not?

8. Prime Minister Klaus states that: "The reforms must be bold, courageous, determined, and therefore, painful. . . . The costs the people have to bear must be widely shared. . . . " Why must the reforms be painful? Why must the pain be widely shared? If the reforms are painful, why carry them out?

9. In 1994, unemployment, virtually unknown under communism, reached 16 percent in Poland, 12 percent in Hungary, and 14 percent in Romania and Ukraine. Why has the transition toward a market economy increased unemployment? Can privatization (selling of state-owned factories to private investors) affect unemployment rates? If so, how?

10. Krystof Prosowski, a Polish worker, said, "I used to feel safe . . . I don't have that feeling any more . . . [In] the past, I used to be paid for eight hours of work every day, no matter how much time I actually spent working . . . What I'm worried about is that if the steel industry as a whole does badly, I could find myself laid off no matter how efficiently I work."* Are such worries an inherent part of a market economy? How can workers reduce them? Do such worries mean that life is better in a planned economy than a free-market economy? Why or why not?

*New York Times, September 30, 1994, p. A10.